ed
and best-known travel brands,
Thomas Cook are the experts in travel.

For more than 135 years our
guidebooks have unlocked the secrets
of destinations around the world,
sharing with travellers a wealth of
experienc assion for travel.

s Cook as your
your next trip
que heritage.

Thomas Cook **pocket** guides

EGYPT
RED SEA RESORTS
Ryan Levitt

[redacted]

thom

1873

Written by Ryan Levitt, updated by Carole French

Published by Thomas Cook Publishing
A division of Thomas Cook Tour Operations Limited
Company registration no. 3772199 England
The Thomas Cook Business Park, Unit 9, Coningsby Road,
Peterborough PE3 8SB, United Kingdom
Email: books@thomascook.com, Tel: +44 (0) 1733 416477
www.thomascookpublishing.com

Produced by Cambridge Publishing Management Limited
Burr Elm Court, Main Street, Caldecote CB23 7NU
www.cambridgepm.co.uk

ISBN: 978-1-84848-546-4

Project Editor: Karen Beaulah
Production/DTP: Steven Collins

Printed and bound in Spain by GraphyCems

CONTENTS

WHAT'S IN YOUR GUIDEBOOK?

Independent authors Impartial, up-to-date information from our travel experts who meticulously source local knowledge.

Experience Thomas Cook's 165 years in the travel industry and guidebook publishing enriches every word with expertise you can trust.

Travel know-how Thomas Cook has thousands of staff working around the globe, all living and breathing travel.

Editors Travel-publishing professionals, pulling everything together to craft a perfect blend of words, pictures, maps and design.

You, the traveller We deliver a practical, no-nonsense approach to information, geared to how you really use it.

Hurghada is one of the most popular resorts

INTRODUCTION
Getting to know Egypt

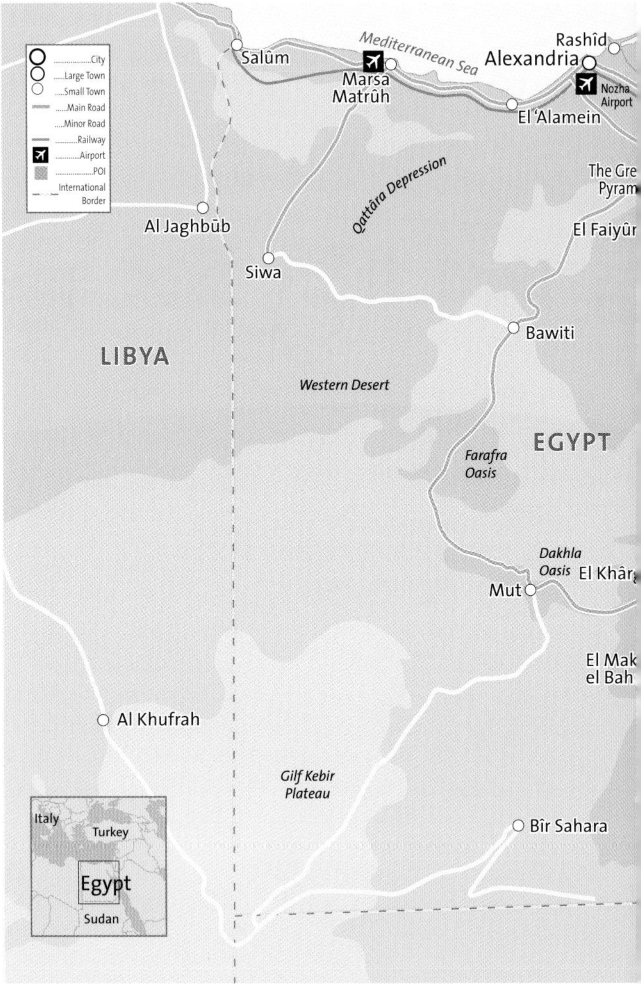
City
Large Town
Small Town
Main Road
Minor Road
Railway
Airport
POI
International Border
Mediterranean Sea
Salûm
Marsa Matrûh
Rashîd
Alexandria
Nozha Airport
El 'Alamein
Qattâra Depression
Al Jaghbūb
Siwa
The Gre
Pyram
El Faiyûr
Bawiti
LIBYA
Western Desert
EGYPT
Farafra Oasis
Dakhla Oasis
El Khâr
Mut
El Mak
el Bah
Al Khufrah
Gilf Kebir Plateau
Bîr Sahara
Italy
Turkey
Egypt
Sudan

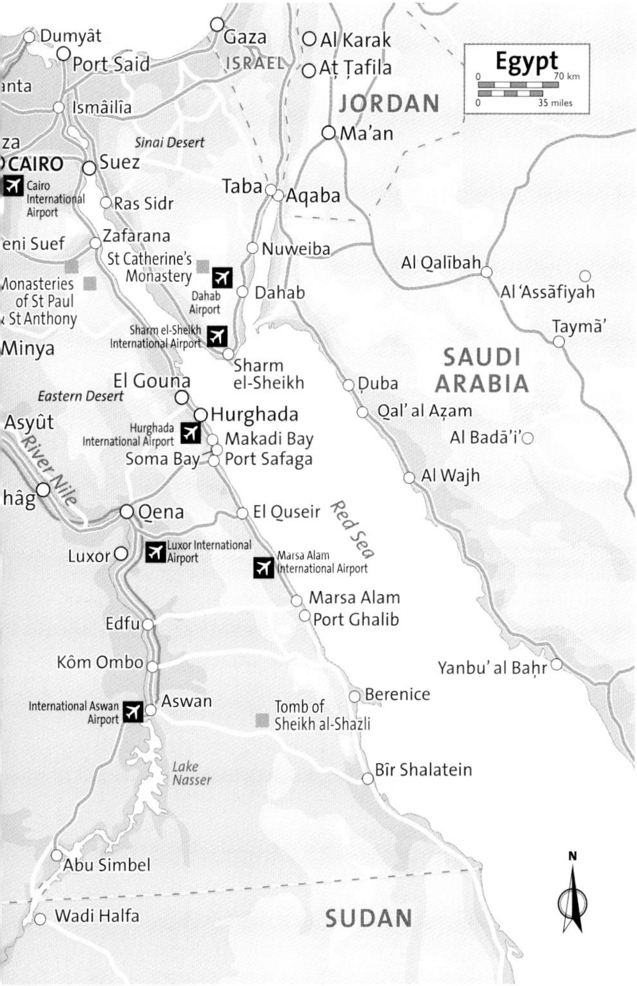
Egypt
0
70 km
0
35 miles
Dumyât
Port Said
Gaza
ISRAEL
Al Karak
Aţ Ţafila
JORDAN
Ismâilîa
Ma'an
Sinai Desert
CAIRO
Suez
Cairo International Airport
Taba
Aqaba
Ras Sidr
Zafarana
Nuweiba
St Catherine's Monastery
Al Qalībah
Dahab Airport
Dahab
Al 'Assāfiyah
Taymā'
Sharm el-Sheikh International Airport
Minya
Sharm el-Sheikh
SAUDI ARABIA
El Gouna
Duba
Eastern Desert
Qal' al Azam
Hurghada
Asyût
Hurghada International Airport
Makadi Bay
Al Badā'i'
Soma Bay
Port Safaga
River Nile
Al Wajh
Qena
El Quseir
Red Sea
Luxor
Luxor International Airport
Marsa Alam International Airport
Marsa Alam
Port Ghalib
Edfu
Kôm Ombo
Yanbu' al Bahr
International Aswan Airport
Aswan
Berenice
Tomb of Sheikh al-Shazli
Lake Nasser
Bîr Shalatein
Abu Simbel
N
Wadi Halfa
SUDAN

Getting to know Egypt

The Red Sea resorts are just a four-hour flight – but a world apart – from the capitals of Europe. Packed with history, charm and fantastic diving opportunities, they have become key winter destinations for sun-seekers from across Britain and beyond. So, down a bottle of beer, plunge into warm, turquoise waters and enjoy a sumptuous meal of Egyptian delights, because your trip to the cradle of civilisation is about to begin.

GEOGRAPHY

Resorts on the Red Sea are divided into two geographical regions: the Sinai peninsula, and the mainland coast, running approximately 1,000 km (620 miles) from Zafarana to the Sudanese border (see map on page 7).

The chief resort on the Sinai peninsula is Sharm el-Sheikh, although the smaller resorts of Dahab, Nuweiba and Taba are also attractive options for the more laid-back holidaymaker. On the mainland coast, Hurghada is the capital of pleasure, with Marsa Alam and El Gouna as popular contenders.

In the Sinai interior, the topography becomes quite mountainous. It is among these great rocks that the ancient stories involving Moses fleeing the Pharaoh through the desert were set. Mount Sinai, for which the peninsula is named, is widely believed to be the location where Moses received the Ten Commandments.

A few kilometres away from the mainland coast are the wilds of the Eastern Desert. This stretch of land is extremely unforgiving, and is dotted with rock paintings left by the nomads of the past.

TRADITIONS & COMMUNITIES

Most Egyptians living in resort towns rely on tourism for their income. Many have moved from other communities in the Nile Valley, drawn by the booming economy. As such, very few can claim to be locals, with the exception of the Bedouin. Although, in the past, Bedouin were suspicious of their traditional lands being taken over in the face of development, a more amicable arrangement evolved economically between Egyptians and Bedouin as the tourist industry grew. Both communities now coexist in the promotion of a welcoming and friendly atmosphere along the coasts of the Red Sea.

LIFESTYLE

Within the arena of North Africa and the Middle East, Egypt is one of the best countries to visit as a tourist. Over the years, Western attitudes have become more accepted in the Sinai and on the Red Sea coast. The tourist industry is valued highly in terms of revenue for Egypt, and although the country has recently undergone major political upheaval, the Egyptians continue to do their utmost to make your visit as enjoyable as possible. Alcohol is widely available in most hotels and restaurants. Bikinis and skimpy clothing are now commonplace on the beaches; however, topless sunbathing is not encouraged, as it is actually illegal in Egypt. Appropriate displays of public affection are not frowned upon, but lewd behaviour is not acceptable. A respectful attitude should have you greeted with a welcoming smile on every corner, as Egyptians tend to pride themselves on their friendly nature and charm.

The beach at Marsa Alam

THE BEST OF THE RED SEA

TOP 10 ATTRACTIONS

- **Marsa Alam** (see page 36), the castle of **Salah ad-Din** (see page 69), and **rock inscriptions** (see page 75) are but a few examples of the area's rich history.

- **The national park at Ras Mohamed** is an area of outstanding beauty (see page 81).

- **St Catherine's Monastery** is a UNESCO World Heritage Site and an important place of pilgrimage for Coptic Christians (see page 84).

- **Camel safaris** provide an insight into the harsh conditions of the Sinai or Eastern Desert (see pages 43, 52 and 86).

- **Visit the ancient temples and tombs at Luxor** for a journey back in time (see page 92).

- **Explore the fascinating resort of Sharm el-Sheikh** with its shopping at the central souk (market) and take a day trip to the nearby Nabq Mangrove Forest (see page 57).

- **Sample the delights of Hurghada**, the nightlife capital on the Red Sea mainland, where you can dive by day and dance till dawn (see page 19).

- **From the well-endowed resort of Marsa Alam**, explore the rocky interior of the Eastern Desert while enjoying the treasures of the Red Sea (see page 36).

- **Learn to dive or improve your diving skills** and explore the beautiful reefs of the **Red Sea** and its many colourful inhabitants (see pages 22, 32 and 59).

- **Hire a guide in the Sinai peninsula** and meet the Bedouin for a fascinating insight into their traditions and lifestyle (see page 45).

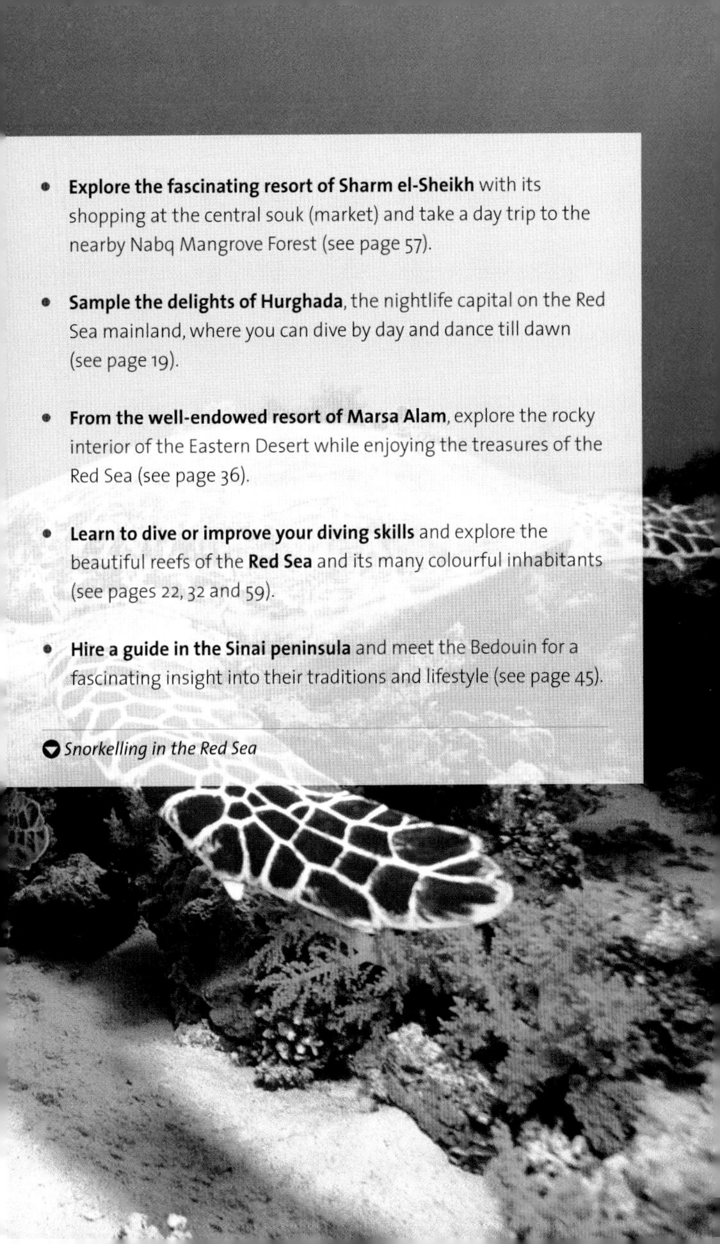

Snorkelling in the Red Sea

SYMBOLS KEY
The following symbols are used throughout this book:

ⓐ address ⓣ telephone ⓦ website address ⓔ email
ⓛ opening times ⓘ important

The following symbols are used on the maps:

𝒊	information office	○	city
✉	post office	○	large town
⬛	shopping	○	small town
✈	airport	⬛	point of interest
✚	hospital	—	main road
⚙	police station		minor road
▭	bus station	—	railway
❶	numbers denote featured	- -	international border
	cafés, restaurants & evening venues		

RESTAURANT CATEGORIES
The symbol after the name of each restaurant listed in this guide
indicates the price of a typical three-course meal without drinks
for one person:
£ under E£50 ££ E£50–100 £££ E£100–200

▶ *Hot, dry Sinai Desert mountains*

RESORTS

Red Sea coast

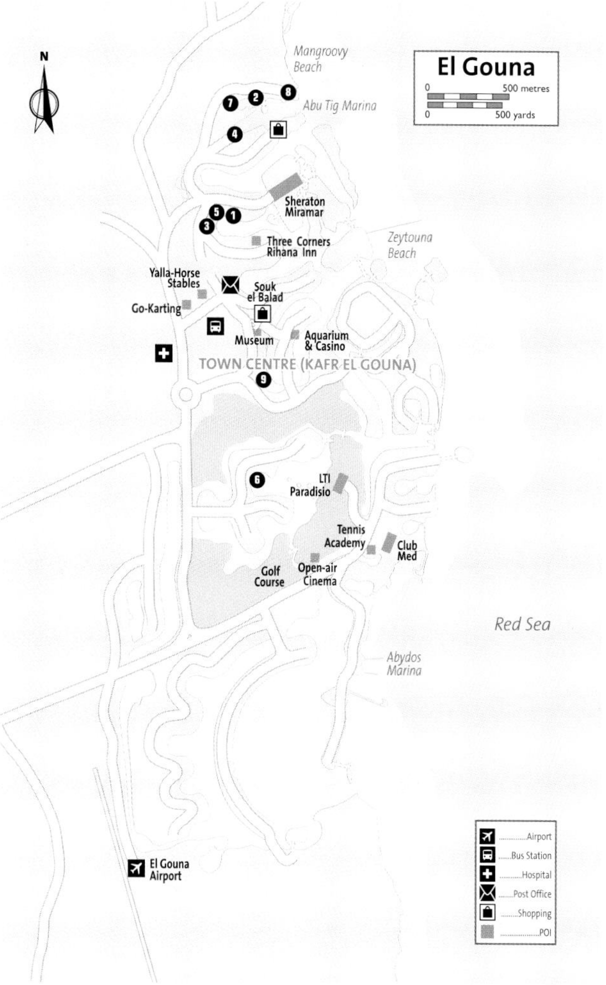
N
El Gouna
0
500 metres
0
500 yards
Mangroovy Beach
Abu Tig Marina
Sheraton Miramar
Three Corners Rihana Inn
Zeytouna Beach
Yalla-Horse Stables
Souk el Balad
Go-Karting
Museum
Aquarium & Casino
TOWN CENTRE (KAFR EL GOUNA)
LTI Paradisio
Tennis Academy
Club Med
Golf Course
Open-air Cinema
Red Sea
Abydos Marina
El Gouna Airport
Airport
Bus Station
Hospital
Post Office
Shopping
POI

El Gouna

This massive resort town is located 22 km (14 miles) north of Hurghada on a chain of islands linked by a series of bridges and canals, and stretches over 11 km (7 miles) of beachfront. It has a visually stunning location set off by the contrast between the red sand of the desert and the turquoise lagoons. The amenities of the ultra-modern Abu Tig Marina are in complete contrast to the traditional feel of the town centre, Kafr El Gouna, with its vibrant bars, restaurants, shops and discos. Don't be fooled by the 'old' feel of the market square, though – everything here was actually built from scratch just a decade or so ago.

El Gouna is home to 10,000 to 15,000 residents comprising a diverse community of entrepreneurs, artists, environmentalists, sport enthusiasts and families. No neon lights or gaudy hotels can be seen on its horizon, everything has been designed and developed to cater to exclusive tastes. Its facilities include a decompression chamber, a library, two shopping areas, a school and a hospital with a plastic surgery centre.

As the tourist destination has thrived, El Gouna has become more self-sufficient by investing in its own brewery, winery and water-bottling company and even a cheese factory. However, its growth has been carefully planned and it won the MENA Golden Award for Best Tourism Project in 2009.

BEACHES

The man-made beaches of El Gouna, some only accessible by boat, are ideal for relaxation and there are numerous dive sites where you can see the splendour of the coral reefs.

Hotels privately own most of the beaches in El Gouna, so if you would like to experience a different stretch of sand from the one your hotel is situated on, you will have to pay a fee. However, although use of a hotel's private beach and facilities (some including lunch) can range from E£60 to E£300, beaches such as Mangroovy and Zeytouna only charge nominal sunbed and towel rental fees.

THINGS TO SEE & DO

Pass the days at El Gouna by booking a dive through the dive centres found at the Sheraton Miramar, Three Corners Rihana Inn or LTI Paradisio Beach and Golf Hotel.

For those who want to do something more than bathe in the rays of sunshine, alternative activities such as tennis, squash, kite-surfing, parasailing and even paintballing are all available. To sample a piece of nomadic lifestyle, Bedouin-led trips are available to the Eastern Desert region.

Children will enjoy a visit to the fish farm, and there is horse riding and go-karting for the older ones. Cheeky Monkeys, a purpose-built indoor play area at the Abu Tig Marina, gives parents a chance to enjoy the delights of the Marina by themselves.

An open-air cinema, aquarium and museum will serve as light entertainment, but for those pursuing night-time partying, there are plenty of restaurants, bars and nightclubs to fulfil their needs.

El Gouna rooftops

TAKING A BREAK

Tamr Henna £–££ ❶ This is a casual outdoor foodcourt in the centre of El Gouna, open daily for breakfast, lunch and dinner. ⓐ Town centre

Maison Thomas ££ ❷ One of a popular chain of restaurants dotted throughout Egypt. Be prepared to experience a generous helping of cheese and fresh ingredients on your pizza. It also serves great sandwiches and salads. ⓐ Abu Tig Marina ⓣ 065 354 55 16 ⓘ Cards accepted

La Tabasco ££ ❸ This popular spot has three terraces with good food. Enjoy music and drinks in an authentic atmosphere. ⓐ Town centre ⓣ 065 358 05 21 ⓘ Cards accepted

Bleu Bleu £££ ❹ International cuisine as well as seafood and local dishes. Has a welcoming atmosphere with a terrace facing the harbour. ⓐ Abu Tig Marina

Jobo's Sports Bar and Restaurant £££ ❺ Located in the heart of El Gouna, this is a great place to people-watch and/or catch sports events. ⓐ Town centre

La Rotisserie £££ ❻ Fine dining in French Mediterranean style. ⓐ Steigenberger Golf Resort ⓣ 065 358 01 40

La Scala £££ ❼ Innovative Italian cuisine. ⓐ Abu Tig Marina

AFTER DARK

Barten ❽ A small bar with modern, funky décor and great atmosphere. ⓐ Abu Tig Marina ⓛ 21.00 until the last person leaves

Dunes ❾ You can choose to sit indoors in a secluded Arabic atmosphere or relax outside in an open Bedouin tent. ⓐ Town centre

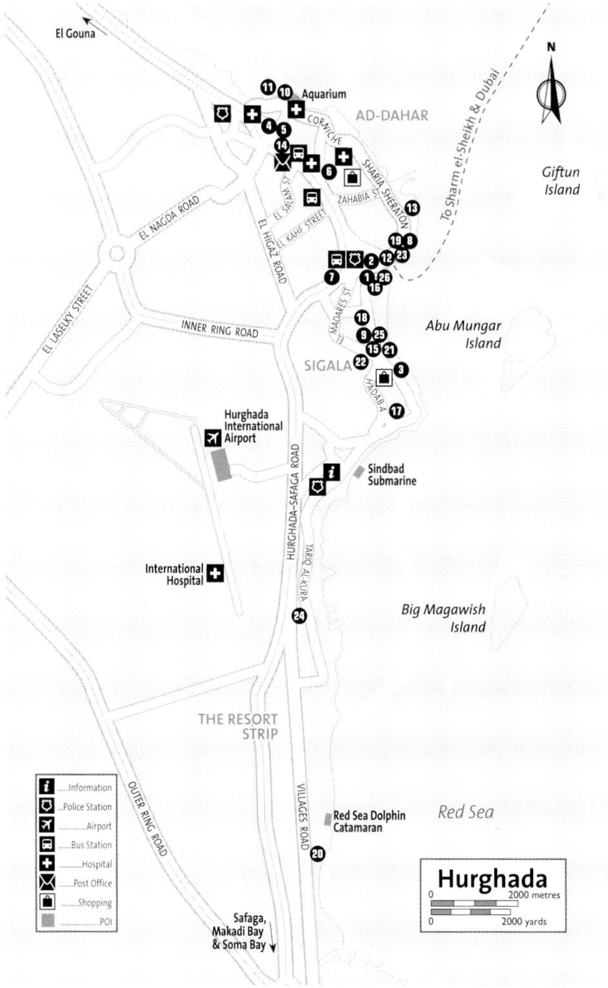
El Gouna
Aquarium
AD-DAHAR
CORNICHE
SHARIA SHERATON
ZAHABIA ST
EL SALAM ST
EL KAHF STREET
EL HIGAZ ROAD
EL NAGDA ROAD
EL LASELKY STREET
INNER RING ROAD
To Sharm el-Sheikh & Dubai
N
Giftun Island
Abu Mungar Island
EL MADARES ST
SIGALA
HADABA
Hurghada International Airport
Sindbad Submarine
HURGHADA–SAFAGA ROAD
TARIQ AL-KURA
International Hospital
Big Magawish Island
THE RESORT STRIP
OUTER RING ROAD
VILLAGES ROAD
Red Sea Dolphin Catamaran
Red Sea
Safaga, Makadi Bay & Soma Bay
Information
Police Station
Airport
Bus Station
Hospital
Post Office
Shopping
POI
Hurghada
0
2000 metres
0
2000 yards

Hurghada

Since the mid-1980s, the town of Hurghada has been transformed from an overlooked fishing village into a booming resort which boasts a population of over 200,000. Through both Egyptian and foreign investment, a conglomerate of more than 100 hotels and resorts has been created, catering to an assortment of tourists ranging from no-star backpackers to five-star hedonists.

With high-quality new properties in Hurghada selling as fast as they are springing up, this has become a red-hot investment spot. An indicator of just how much growth this area is experiencing is the extensive renovation work that has been carried out at Hurghada airport to cope with the rise in traffic. Hurghada itself is still seeing a great deal of development work in several areas along the coast, particularly around its new marina, close to the popular Arabia Beach resorts.

Set against a backdrop of designer yachts, the Marina Boulevard, opened in 2008, accommodates stylish apartments, as well as over 100 outlets ranging from popular retail shops to trendy cafés, restaurants and bars.

For children, there is a purpose-built indoor play area, Cheeky Monkeys, with childcare facilities, so you can drop 'n' shop!

Further expansion is ongoing in the already newly developed promenade area of El Kawser, with its array of bars, restaurants, shops and diving centres. An enormous new development is also planned at Gamsha Bay, north of the town, encompassing not only luxury accommodation but also entertainment venues, theme parks and golf courses, all attracting further investment to the region.

Attracted by the beckoning call of hot sun and warm waters, the emerging Russian middle class availed themselves en masse of the opportunity of cheap flights and package deals, and you may encounter such Russian delicacies as *borscht* on some menus to demonstrate Hurghada's loyalty to their consistent migration to their shores.

The resort has three main areas, all of which you are bound to visit at some point during your holiday.

Ad-Dahar

Ad-Dahar is the oldest part of Hurghada, containing the town's liveliest bazaar. It is where almost all of the budget accommodation can be found. It's in the northern end of town at the end of a long stretch of resorts that crowd the neighbourhood. Many of the buildings remain unfinished and are on unpaved streets.

The resort strip

South of Sigala, a road winds along the coast through the resort strip, and this is where most of the five-star properties are located. Some 15 km (9 miles) south of Ad-Dahar, the road meets another inland. This marks the beginning of Hurghada's major development of new resorts which are in various stages of completion and stretch as far as Safaga. If you're looking for a change of pace, this road continues to Makadi Bay and Soma Bay – two luxury destinations along the coast.

Sigala

This is the fastest-growing part of the town. Separated from Ad-Dahar by a lengthy road, it is packed with resorts that vie for a slice of sea frontage. Back from the beach are two- and three-star properties that are less lucky in their location. The main street is Sharia Sheraton, named after the resort that brought success to Sigala. Here you'll find most of the best restaurants, loads of shops and a lively crowd, day or night. If you plan to travel on to Sharm el-Sheikh or Dubai, ferries depart from the main passenger port.

BEACHES

Although there is a public beach in Sigala, it is quite stark and surrounded by development. Western women sunbathing will also find themselves subject to invasive stares and hassle from local men. The best option for enjoying the sand and sea is to avail yourself of the resort's private beaches, most of which charge a fee between E£20 and E£60 for beach access to non-residents.

Tourism is what Hurghada is now about, accounting for more than 95 per cent of the local economy. However, the bid to boost the town coffers has come at a price. The once pristine waters are no longer as clean as they used to be, and some of the coral reefs close to the coast that formerly beckoned divers with their beauty have been almost destroyed.

Wonderful marine life can be seen during a dive in the Red Sea around [redacted]

THINGS TO SEE & DO

Aquarium

You may recognise some of the Red Sea fish and other marine creatures here. Tanks are labelled in English, so it is a good place for children, although some of the tanks (and specimens) look a little worse for wear. ⓐ Corniche, Ad-Dahar ⓣ 065 354 85 57 ⓛ 09.00–23.00 daily ⓘ Admission charge

Diving

Although there are many diving operators that offer top-quality experiences on the Red Sea coast, it is important that you always check your instructor's credentials before going on a dive. Your life may depend on it! Just remember, photocopies of an ID and insurance are not necessarily valid representations of their qualifications.

Ironically, though diving is originally what attracted tourism to Hurghada, its consequent development in the beginning damaged a lot of the reefs off the mainland. In 1999 recognised damage to the coral reefs of Giftun Island prompted a E£45-million preservation plan to protect the coastal environs and coral reefs near Hurghada and south along the Red Sea coast. **HEPCA** (Hurghada Environmental Protection and Conservation Association) actively works towards protecting and preserving the natural resources of the Red Sea and Egypt. It has installed mooring buoys in a number of dive sites, discourages the practices of coral and shell collection by tourists, organises underwater and beach clean-ups and campaigns to stop overfishing to protect endangered marine life. In 2004 it successfully campaigned to save Giftun Island, well known as a major nesting ground for green turtles, from a US$2-billion tourism development plan. As a result, there are still many unspoilt coral reefs and great diving opportunities to be found on the offshore islands south of Hurghada.

A typical four- or five-day PADI open-water course from a reputable diving centre should cost £240–360 (US$380–580), including the certificate. A two-day advanced course will be £170–260 (US$270–420). Introductory dives are available for those who want to sample the idea of exploring the underwater world for £21–34 (US$30–50). Similarly, the Bubblemaker dive gives children as young as eight a first-hand experience of the reefs for £20–50 (US$30–80). Scuba equipment should be included in the package price. For qualified divers, a day of boat diving averages £25–35 (US$40–60) and should include a minimum of two dives.

Enthusiastic divers frustrated by the limitations of one-day dive trips will be attracted by the idea of living aboard a vessel for periods generally ranging from two days to two weeks to access a greater range of dive sites. A minimum of six people is usually required to set sail, so, although it is possible to arrange these mini-safaris once you arrive at your resort, it is recommended that you book in advance through an agency or online. Before setting sail, it is important to check that the boat is equipped in accordance with safety guidelines (in other words, that it has a radio, lifejackets, oxygen and a first-aid kit).

You can find a full list of member dive centres on the HEPCA website. 065 344 50 35 www.hepca.com

There are dozens of dive sites within a day's journey from Hurghada. Some of the better ones include:

Abu Ramada Just off Giftun Island, this dive site is okay if you are looking for fish, but far more interesting if you prefer coral. There are three coral blocks here dripping with eye-poppingly bright soft corals.

Careless Reef Accessible only in calm weather, but definitely worth any wait. See whitetip sharks and moray eels fight and mate around this plateau. It has an inspiring drop-off and Eden-like gardens of table and soft corals.

El-Aruk Gigi Delightful reef with seven ergs (dune fields) including large table corals. One of the easiest sites to access from Hurghada.

Gota Abu Ramada A great spot to view spotted gropers, bannerfish and sweetlips. Keep an eye out for standing ergs and 1,500-year-old stony corals. In 2007 the first Shark Monument was placed underwater nearby as part of a worldwide campaign in cooperation with the international shark protection organisation SHARKPROJECT and HEPCA.

Samadai Reef ('Dolphin House') This horseshoe-shaped reef is better for snorkellers, but as the area is used by dolphins as a nursery it is well worth the trip. Buoys are installed to ensure no boats get in and disturb the newborns.

Sha'ab Petra Contains a small coral formation, which is home to a great variety of fish colonies. Pay close attention to the large holes in the ergs with their abundance of interesting marine and coral life.

Sha'ab Sabrina Located off Giftun Island, there lies a beautiful hard coral garden containing a diverse array of marine life including moray and yellow mouth eels, butterfly fish, lionfish, green turtles and the occasional dolphin if you are lucky.

Red Sea Dolphin Catamaran

A great way to experience the Red Sea's underwater life. The Dolphin is a two-hour ride with panoramic views of the coral reefs and fish. ⓐ Hilton Hurghada Long Beach Resort Aqua Centre ⓣ 065 346 32 43

Sindbad Submarine

Take your aquatic adventure a step further! Tours by submarine dive to 22 m (72 ft), designed mostly as a photo opportunity. The trip takes two hours, half of it spent getting to and from the dive site. Once submerged, a diver swims along the side trailing bait to attract fish. ⓐ Bookings can be made at the Sindbad Beach Resort ⓣ 065 344 96 01 ⓘ Admission charge

TAKING A BREAK

Abu Khadega £ ❶ If you want to try basic Egyptian workers' grub, then this is the place to do it. Go for the excellent *kofta* and the chance to mix with locals. Good if you're on a tight budget. ⓐ Near the police station in Sigala Square ⓣ 065 344 37 68 ⓘ Cash only

Café del Mar £ ❷ An extensive selection of salads and local dishes with an emphasis on seafood greets you at this popular café. ⓐ Off Arousa Square ⓣ 010 071 67 71

El-Arabi £ ❸ Local favourite known for its 'Eastern' food. Dishes are good value. ⓐ Sharia Sheraton, opposite the Seagull Hotel ⓣ 065 344 03 77 ⓘ Cash only

Pizza Tarboush £ ❹ Shop in the souk and then drop in to this busy pizza parlour serving up decent pizza with a variety of toppings. ⓐ Sharia Abdel Aziz Mustafa ⓣ 065 354 84 56 ⓘ Cash only

Young Kang £ ❺ Surprisingly tasty Chinese–Korean eatery. The place is tiny, but everyone manages to make do in the confined space. Basics like fried rice and sweet-and-sour pork are your best options. Beer is also served. ⓐ Sharia Sheikh Sabak ⓣ 012 422 93 27 ⓘ Cash only

Hard Rock Cafe £–££ ❻ Whether it's a club sandwich or a mouthwatering cocktail you're after, or you simply want to relax to live music, the Hard Rock won't disappoint. ⓐ Tareek el Kora ⓣ 065 346 51 70 ⓦ www.hardrock.com/hurghada

Hefny Seafood Restaurant £–££ ❼ Here is your chance to sample the fruits of the sea at affordable prices. Wide variety of fish freshly caught that day is sold by weight and served with salads and rice. You can dine in or order takeaway. ⓐ Sharia Mina ⓣ 065 344 52 98 ⓘ Cash only

Bordiehn's ££ ❽ Divine international dishes with a sense of creativity exceeding most other menus in town. Ingredients are fresh (try camel meat!) even if the atmosphere is a bit lacking. It has a sister venue called B's at the marina. ⓐ Arabella Azur resort ⓣ 065 354 87 90

Relaxing at Hurghada

Bulls Steakhouse ££ ❾ Missing meat? Look no further; the Bulls menu is a temple for carnivores. Chinese dishes, if less successful, are also on offer. ⓐ Sharia Sheraton ⓣ 065 344 44 14

Cacao Bar ££ ❿ Previously known as La Scarabeo, but still under the same ownership, they adhere to their old menu of pizzas, pasta and oregano-dusted bread with the addition of steaks and chicken. Entertainment comes in the form of live bands playing Mondays and Thursdays, as well as a big flat screen to cater to football enthusiasts. ⓐ Sharia Sayyed al-Qorayem ⓣ 012 618 48 61 ! Cash only

Chez Pascal ££ ⓫ Delightful bistro that serves European cuisine. Enjoy the sea bass or steak, while relaxing in sunny surroundings. ⓐ Sharia Sayyed al-Qorayem ⓣ 065 336 51 87

Joker ££ ⓬ Great seafood restaurant with excellent squid. Portion sizes are generous, so it's worth working up an appetite. ⓐ Near the police station in Sigala Square ⓣ 065 354 31 46 ! Cash only

Moby Dick ££ ⓭ This cosy restaurant decorated in an exotic Egyptian style serves local dishes – be sure to try the tasty camel steaks. ⓐ Sharia Sheraton ⓣ 065 344 00 51 ⓦ www.mobydick-egypt.com

Red Sea Restaurant ££ ⓮ When a package tourist decides to go off-resort, this is the place they head for. Seafood dishes are recommended. ⓐ Sharia An-Nasr ⓣ 065 354 77 04

Rossi's ££ ⓯ Italian dishes, especially good for crispy pizza; the pasta is hit or miss. Stick with the basics and you'll do fine. ⓐ Sharia Sheraton, opposite the now-defunct Aquafun waterpark ⓣ 065 344 60 12

Starfish ££ ⓰ A family restaurant located right on the main strip. Speciality is seafood, but there's a good range of grills and salads too. ⓐ Off Sharia Sheraton ⓣ 065 344 37 50

Da Nanni **££–£££** ⓱ The best oven-baked pizzas and mouthwatering pasta dishes in town are served in this upbeat restaurant owned by an Italian couple and inspired by the best of Italy. ⓐ Sharia Al-Hadaba ⓣ 065 344 70 18 ⓦ www.dananni.net

Alexanders **£££** ⓲ This elegant restaurant specialises in Mediterranean and French cuisine in classic surroundings. Dine on the veranda overlooking the sea or stay in the colonial-style dining room. Reservations required. ⓐ Steigenberger Al Dau Beach Hotel, Youssif Afifi Road ⓣ 065 346 54 00 ⓦ www.steigenbergeraldaubeach.com

Pita Sphinx **£££** ⓳ Elegant and serving gourmet European cuisine with an Egyptian twist, the Pita Sphinx is the place to be seen. Specialities include chargrilled salmon and chicken with a pineapple salsa. ⓐ Sharia Sheraton ⓣ 065 344 91 05 ⓦ www.pitasphinx.com

AFTER DARK

Alf Layla wa Layla ⓴ If you like your entertainment to be kitsch with a capital 'K', then this is for you. Described as a 'belly-dancing extravaganza', a brightly coloured show features Russian belly-dancers swaying their way across a stage festooned with lights, dazzle and glitz. Not the place for those looking for an authentic introduction to this Middle Eastern dance form. ⓐ Villages Road ⓣ 065 346 46 02 ❶ Cards accepted

Buda Ramoza Beach Club ㉑ An in-house DJ provides the music, while you feast on marinated delicacies from the barbecue. They host Sunday Sunset sessions giving you an opportunity to relax in the pool or rock-pool whirlpool, while sipping sundowners. ⓐ Buddha Beach ⓣ 011 182 81 11/010 229 22 13 ⓦ www.budaramozaclub.com ❶ Cash only

Calypso ㉒ This purpose-built bunker is perhaps known more for its crowds of female Russian tourists than for any hip resident DJs. The international cultural show is best avoided. ⓐ Sharia Al-Hadaba ⓣ 065 344 95 83 ❶ Cards accepted

Hed Kandi Beach Bar (HKV001) ㉓ Formerly known as the Chill and Liquid Lounge, this a great hangout for divers and foreign revellers who like to chill on the beach, relax in the hot tub or dance by the pool. Full moon parties and Hed Kandi LIVE events are popular dates in the month. ⓐ Marina Boulevard ⓣ 016 883 35 53 ❶ Cash only

Little Buddha ㉔ Expensive restaurant, sushi bar and lounge which transforms into a club with DJ at 23.30. Modern zen-like incense-filled surroundings with an extensive cocktail list. ⓐ Sindbad Beach Resort, Villages Road ⓣ 065 345 01 20 ⓦ www.littlebuddha-hurghada.com ❶ Cards accepted

Papas Bar ㉕ Dutch-run drinking spot that is favoured by the diving crowd. ⓐ Sharia Sheraton, next to Rossi's ⓣ 010 512 90 51 ❶ Cash only

Papas Beach Club ㉖ Now licensed by the international clubbing brand Ministry of Sound, it caters to a variety of tastes and features popular DJ events, live music and big-screen sports. It also has a new food menu. ⓐ Marina Boulevard ⓣ 016 883 35 54 ⓦ www.papasbar.com

Makadi Bay & Soma Bay

South of Hurghada are two sandy bays worth a visit. The first is Makadi Bay and the second, further south, is Soma Bay, both rapidly expanding.

Makadi Bay, a popular modern beach resort set on a wide sandy bay situated against a backdrop of desert dunes, is located 33 km (20 miles) south of Hurghada. It is a relatively small bay with good all-inclusive family hotels. Tourists choose to come here to relax, as it is mainly a quiet holiday destination. When you feel up to venturing off hotel grounds, be sure to check out Souk Makadi, which has a variety of shops selling everything from jewellery to pure perfume oils and high-quality cotton clothing.

A similarly tranquil destination, 45 km (28 miles) south of Hurghada, Soma Bay houses five hotels with one more presently in the pipeline. As it expands, the bay aspires to meet a variety of interests. La Résidence des Cascades is a golfer's haven, with an 18-hole award-winning golf course with a spa and thalassic therapy centre inspired by the availability of black sand in the region.

Overlooking the 'Marsa Tubaya' Marina, there is a small village called **El Khan**, where you will find some street cafés and local wares including a handicraft centre selling Bedouin jewellery. A commercial and entertainment centre can be found at the Marina. Here, different dining options are available in the form of quayside cafés, bars and restaurants.

THINGS TO SEE & DO

The bays provide an excellent location for some great Red Sea water activities like kite-surfing and windsurfing. Activities such as sand buggy desert excursions and quad biking, as well as horse and camel riding, are also available.

Almost all activities are resort and hotel based, but day or overnight trips to Luxor and the monasteries of St Anthony and St Paul can easily be organised. For those with a taste for adventure, there is an overnight trip to the desert, which includes a night camping underneath the stars and time with a Bedouin tribe. There are boat trips to an abundance of local reefs and islands with several wrecks and more challenging reef dives to suit more experienced divers. Other attractive options include embarking on deep-sea fishing trips, or excursions in glass-bottom boats, in the hope of spotting the sharks, giant eels, manta rays and tuna that inhabit the Red Sea.

Modern resort hotels overlook the sea at Makadi Bay

Port Ghalib

Port Ghalib is the first official private seaport of entry into Egypt and is evolving into a thriving community. Home to one of the largest man-made lagoons in the world, it is presently composed of four international hotels, a diving lodge, a marina and a convention centre. Located just ten minutes from Marsa Alam International Airport, tourists can expect a fast transit to the holiday of their choice, whether it's lounging by the pool or sampling a myriad of water-based activities.

Port Ghalib is a literal oasis in the desert beside the sea, with large areas still undeveloped, so you can expect a quiet holiday with no massive influx of noisy travellers. The four-star Marina Lodge is on one side of the marina, while the other three InterContinental-franchised hotels are on the other. However, whichever hotel you choose to reside in, you can expect to have full access to the facilities of the others, leaving you with a choice of pools, a jetty to snorkel from and a beach to relax on, as well as the various restaurants contained within the resort itself.

THINGS TO SEE & DO

Currently, Port Ghalib is most noted for its diving and snorkelling prospects, as well as offering a peaceful environment to relax in. Behind the luxurious sea-facing apartments, there is a souk with the customary shopkeepers vying for your trade.

The hotels also offer extensive sport and leisure activities, including quad biking, camel rides and desert safaris. You can even grab the chance to visit fabulous ancient sites like the Valley of the Kings and Queens, Karnak and the Luxor temples, as these are merely two and a half hours away.

Diving

Port Ghalib is seeing enormous growth in the volume of safari dive boats embarking from the marina. After many years of Sharm el-Sheikh and Hurghada being the main places to be, divers are starting to move on to newer underwater pastures like Port Ghalib. Some of the world's most spectacular dive sites are within easy reach of the resort and are renowned for their reefs and unique marine ecosystem, which are home to both hard and soft corals and a great variety of marine life including sharks, turtles and dolphins. **Emperor Divers** offers boat diving, with some shore diving, depending on conditions. ⓐ Marina Lodge ⓣ 012 737 21 26 ⓦ www.emperordivers.com

Daedalus Reef A huge round reef with a lighthouse more than 64 km (40 miles) away from the coast with excellent chances to spot big pelagics including manta rays. All around its steep walls you will see an extreme variety of fish and coral. Good chance to see schooling hammerheads on the northern point too.

Elphinstone Reef A large cigar-shaped offshore reef which offers exhilarating and spectacular wall diving with regular sightings of large pelagics including oceanic whitetip sharks, tuna and barracuda, as well as hammerheads, napoleons and turtles. Richly decorated with soft corals, sponges, gorgonians and fans.

Marsa Mubarak The largest dive site with seven wildly different diving experiences offering the chance to see everything from puffer fish to dugongs, giant green sea turtles to trunk fishes and everything in-between. With sea grass, pinnacles, coral gardens and reef walls, this dive site gives you the opportunity to see just about all the flora and fauna the Red Sea has to offer.

Dolphin safaris

The dolphin reef is regulated by the marine park rangers, who have sectioned off three parts of it to protect the dolphins' natural environment. One is for the dolphins themselves, the second for snorkellers and the third is a drop-off point for the boats. The dolphins swim in and out of all sections, sometimes coming right up to the boats.

They tend to be in groups and are usually easily spotted from the boat, but you need to swim slowly towards them and not try to catch hold of them. Remember to bring an underwater camera with you. ! Divers are not allowed in the area, but can come to enjoy the excellent dive sites outside the reef

Lulee Kids Camp

Situated on the campus of The Palace, Crowne Plaza Sahara Sands and Sahara Oasis, Lulee Kids Camp offers a supervised range of activities, such as treasure hunts, mini-golf and bumper boats for children at 2–12 years old (high season) and 4–12 years old (low season).
t 065 336 00 00 w www.intercontinental.com/portghalib

Snorkelling

The marina has two coral beach areas: the southern beach is ideal for swimming, while the eastern beach offers access via two piers to the reefs that surround the resort. The beach is very clean and there is always someone from the hotels around to serve you refreshments. If you snorkel between the two piers, turtles, dolphins and octopus abound, while the beach house reef is a wonderful nursery for different types of fish.

You can organise trips through your hotel or with dive centres such as Emperor Divers (see page 33).

TAKING A BREAK

Restaurants and bars are self-contained within the resort, but there are plans in the future to further develop the promenade on the Corniche into a stretch of retail outlets, restaurants, cafés and bars with a cinema and theatre. If you care to wander down there now, you will find approximately 25 outlets, including a few American fast-food restaurants, a couple of coffee places, a small modern café with a flat-screen TV, ATMs, a supermarket and some gift shops. Two notable hotel-based restaurants are:

Budours Court £££ The restaurant offers elegant Moroccan fare in a traditional setting on the Corniche. Plays music for its guests in the evenings. ⓐ Corniche ⓣ 065 336 00 00

The Olive Restaurant £££ This upmarket restaurant is located on the upper level of a garden terrace overlooking the sea. Expect to be spoilt by a medley of Arabic and Mediterranean dishes. ⓐ The Palace InterContinental ⓣ 065 336 00 00

Marsa Alam

Once upon a time, Marsa Alam was just a remote fishing village located 132 km (82 miles) south of El Quseir. The town itself is just a few buildings surrounded by an army base, but its shores became a secret excursion for experienced divers who wanted to venture into unexplored depths. As the word spread to the Ministry of Tourism, a new international airport emerged along with many new resorts.

ANCIENT HISTORY

For thousands of years there has been a road from Marsa Alam to the temple village of Edfu, 230 km (143 miles) across the desert to the west. The current paved road follows the line of an ancient trail that was originally built by Ptolemy II and linked the Nile Valley with the Red Sea. Emeralds and gold were mined in the region, making it a rich revenue source for the Pharaohs. Criminals and political prisoners were worked

A view over the waters off Marsa Alam's unspoilt reef-lined coast

literally to death under the searing rays of the sun. Precious jewels have since been replaced by phosphate, though the mining way of life remains hard. To travel on the paved desert road between Marsa Alam and Edfu, you must be accompanied by a guide or an experienced tour operator. Some roads still require a guarded convoy to ensure safety.

THINGS TO SEE & DO

Desert safaris

For trips into the desert, **Red Sea Desert Adventures** is a company run by a Dutch geologist and her partner. The two have lived in Marsa Alam for over a decade and are authorities on the art and culture of local Ababda tribespeople. Tours are tailor-made and can include walking, camel rides or jeep explorations throughout the area. ⓣ 012 399 38 60 ⓦ www.redseadesertadventures.com

Diving

The best dive centre worth organising a trip with is the **Red Sea Diving Safari**, a tour operator committed to the protection of the local environment. It is possible to stay on-site, although accommodation tends to be extremely basic – we're talking tents and stone huts. ⓣ 023 337 18 33 (Cairo office) ⓦ www.redsea-divingsafari.com

Deep South diving centre, 14 km (nearly 9 miles) south of town, offers trips to the best and most remote dive sites in the south, including Elphinstone, Fury Shoal, Dolphin House and Abu Dahab. The price of open-water diving courses can be negotiated. ⓣ 012 792 33 36 ⓦ www.deep-south-diving.com ⓔ karim@deep-south-diving.com

The *moulid*

A *moulid* is a religious festival that celebrates the birthday of a local saint or holy person. It usually lasts a week and reaches its climax with the *Leila Kebira* ('big night'). Over 60,000 Sufis from across the country gather to perform *zikrs* (Koranic verses), and hundreds of tents and market stalls are pitched.

SHARK ATTACKS

Shark attacks in Marsa Alam are quite rare; indeed the last fatal attack was in 2009 when a snorkeller was killed at a remote diving spot, St John's reef. More recently, however, there have been some sightings, and you are advised not to aggravate the sharks or give them food.

The tomb of Sayyed al-Shazli

Approximately 145 km (90 miles) southwest of Marsa Alam is the tomb of the 13th-century Sheikh Sayyed al-Shazli, an important Sufi leader, who was buried here due to his desire to die where no one had ever sinned. According to legend, the Prophet Muhammad heard his prayer and personally selected this remote desert location.

In 1947 King Farouk restored the tomb and made it easier to reach by constructing an asphalt road. During periods of heightened security, however, checkpoints may sometimes turn you back.

Whirling dervishes

If you plan on attending the *moulid* in the hopes of seeing the famous Sufi whirling dervishes, you may be disappointed. Whirling dervishes follow a branch of Sufism which was founded in Turkey. This branch has never really taken off in Egypt and in fact is sometimes thought of as blasphemous by orthodox Muslims. Other Sufi orders boast much wider support. Stick to the tourist-focused shows in Cairo if you want to see the twirling in action.

TAKING A BREAK

At present, the range of dining and drinking establishments in Marsa Alam is extremely limited. You will be restricted to the facilities of the various hotels – usually an 'international' restaurant serving local and European cuisine, and a small disco.

Jeep safari through the Sinai Desert run by Bedouin

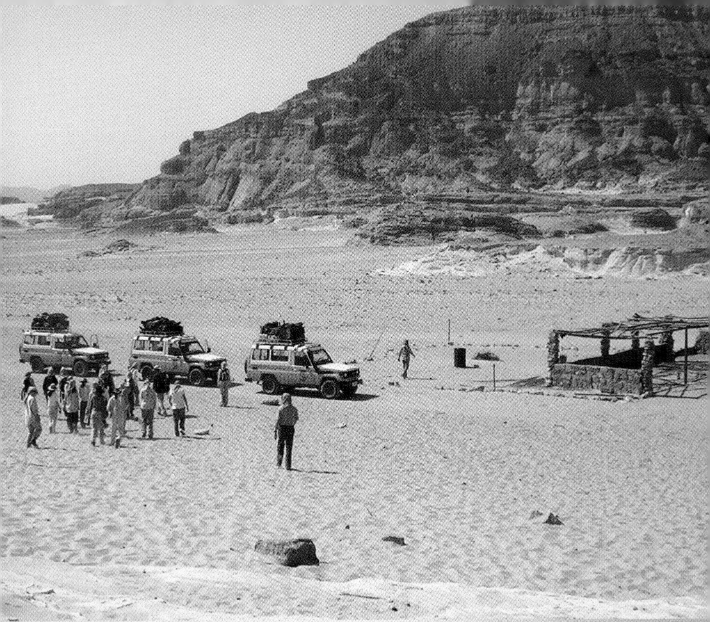

RESORTS
Sinai peninsula

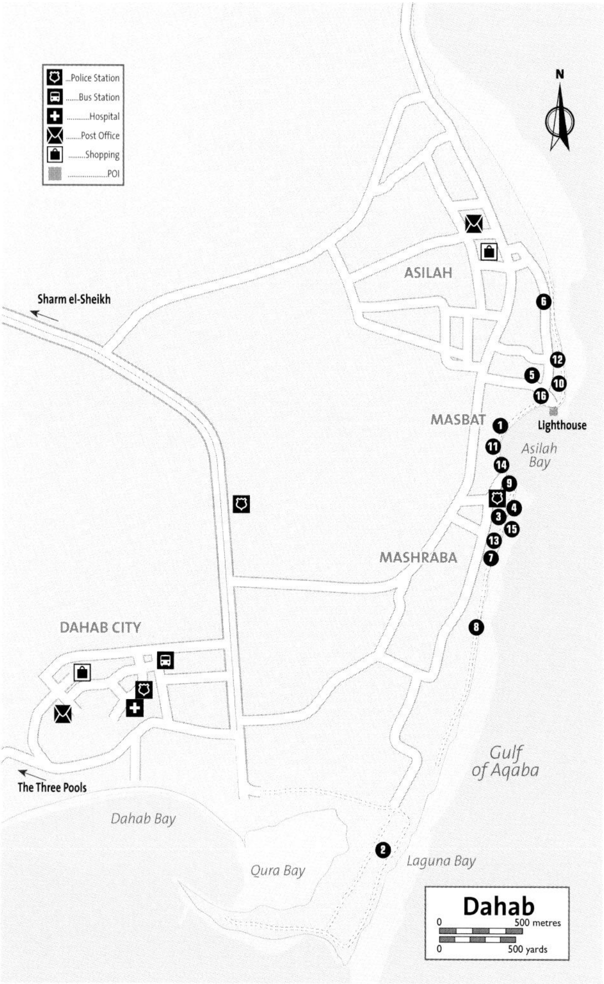
...Police Station
.......Bus Station
............Hospital
........Post Office
........Shopping
....................POI
N
ASILAH
Sharm el-Sheikh
MASBAT
Lighthouse
Asilah Bay
MASHRABA
DAHAB CITY
Gulf of Aqaba
The Three Pools
Dahab Bay
Laguna Bay
Qura Bay
Dahab
0
500 metres
0
500 yards

Dahab

Jagged mountains meet a turquoise sea at a series of tawny beaches known as Dahab, located 95 km (59 miles) north of Sharm el-Sheikh. The name 'Dahab' is derived from the Arabic word for 'gold', an apt name drawn from the glow of the golden sands that stretch as far as the eye can see. It's an intriguing resort town that has evolved from its bohemian beginnings but has managed to avoid the massive-complex mentality of Sharm el-Sheikh, retaining its identity with a sense of maturity and spreading its relaxed atmosphere evenly among the holiday villages and younger, more adventurous travellers.

Asilah

The main tourist stretch and most atmospheric part of Dahab is the original Bedouin settlement of Asilah that runs north along the beach.

From its humble beginnings as a Bedouin enclave and spot of rest and relaxation for the Israeli troops in the 1960s, the town has evolved into the preferred carefree seaside resort for the independent traveller. With a paved boardwalk that marks the beachfront, the village is now home to an expanding series of hotels, diving centres and beach restaurants. As well as serviced apartments, you will find a delightful boutique hotel nestled away from the seafront, **Dahab Paradise**.
ⓣ 010 700 25 27 ⓦ www.dahabparadise.com

Dahab City

This small area, consisting of a bus station, a post office, a bank and a few interspersed hotels, will be of little significance to the traveller, who will glimpse it momentarily when disembarking from the bus before catching a taxi headed for the village.

Masbat

The curved part that rings the bay, Masbat is the original downtown centre and was a hippy haven in the 1980s and '90s. It remains the bustling part of the town with a stretch of restaurants dating back to its beginnings as a tourist destination. A small pedestrian bridge marks the centre of the town where there is a busy bazaar. The shopfronts have changed slightly but give no real visible sign of the bombing that took place in 2006 during the Sham el-Nessim public holiday. Expect to encounter a good degree of hassle from pushy restaurateurs.

Mashraba

As you walk south of Masbat, past the police station, you will encounter Mashraba, a myriad of different restaurants along with their affiliated dive centres and hotels. If you fancy a massage or pampering, beachside tents offering various indulgent choices will beckon amid the sea breeze.

BEACHES

If you don't fancy wearing swimming shoes to protect you from the stabbing sensation of the coral, the laguna area of Mashraba has a

A street lined with restaurants in Mashraba

HEALTH & HAPPINESS

Due to major crackdowns, the days of Dahab being a hashish haven are at an end. An infamous old hash trafficking point is now occupied by a police station. Dope-smoking in Egypt can result in jail sentences or heavy fines.

delightful stretch of soft sand. Owned by the five-star resorts situated there, you can still partake for E£45 a day (including breakfast in the Meridian or the Hilton). It is an ideal site for windsurfing. The southern side is continually expanding outwards to the picturesque setting of the mountains, with future plans for more environmentally friendly wind- and solar-powered hotels.

THINGS TO SEE & DO

Camel & jeep safaris

For a short trip along the beach, you can rent camels, or horses if you are happy to pay more. Longer trips are just as easy to arrange, thanks to a plethora of guides. Try to find a Bedouin guide as they know more than a transplanted Egyptian. Guiding is also a major source of revenue for the Bedouin community. Look for camel drivers along the waterfront, but don't pay the camel driver until you return to town.

Most safari companies can offer trips to the interior and try to promote local culture. Even if you don't want a formal tour, they are still a great source for private guides. Try Embah Safari Tours and King Safari (see page 107).

Specific locations that are offered on itineraries to the interior are the Coloured Canyon and Nabq Mangrove Forest (see pages 53, 78 and 80).

Diving

While dive sites aren't as filled with fish as those off Sharm or Hurghada, there are several locations well worth exploring. Shore diving is the norm, with reefs reached by pickups. The best are north of Dahab Bay, just past the lagoon. Asilah offers fewer options, except for the area around the lighthouse. Most divers in the know head 7–8 km (around 5 miles) up the coast to Eel Garden, Canyon and Blue Hole.

Daily trips to these sites can be arranged through almost every dive centre. Three of the better ones are **Fantasea Red Sea** (ⓣ 069 364 11 95 ⓦ www.fantasearedsea.com), **Big Blue Dahab** (ⓣ 069 364 00 45 ⓦ www.bigbluedahab.com) and **Orca Dive Club** (ⓣ 017 512 04 44 ⓦ www.orca-diveclub-dahab.com). Choose your club carefully as some of the centres have poor safety standards. Ask around if you are unsure.

Blue Hole For experienced divers, the Blue Hole is the challenge of a lifetime. Every year, this incredible site claims several lives. It's a spectacular shaft that at its deepest plunges to 130 m (425 ft). The challenge involves descending 60 m (197 ft) and swimming through a transverse passage to come up on the other side. Divers who ascend too quickly risk 'the bends'. If you worry about your skill level, stay close to the surface and work your way around to a dip in the reef known as the Bridge. There's plenty to see – even at shallow depths; however, the Blue Hole is so popular now that snorkellers seem to have become more abundant than fish. ❗ Warning: inexperienced divers should not attempt this dive

Canyon The Canyon is a dark, narrow fissure reached by swimming along the reef from the shore and then diving to the edge of a coral wall. Inexperienced divers should not attempt this dive as it sinks to a depth of 50 m (164 ft). If you do want to dive the Canyon, there is still plenty to see at the top of the reef.

Eel Garden There are many sand eels here, as well as beautiful coral walls. Dives can sometimes be tricky because of the wind, so they require good diving weather.

Ras Abu Gallum This protected area, a 30-km (19-mile) stretch of coastline with three diving beaches accessed by jeep or camel, is the main day-long dive destination, with deep virgin reefs with a variety of corals and fish.

The Three Pools If you would like a less tourist-populated area to snorkel or dive, a short distance south of Dahab lies the Bedouin oasis called 'The Three Pools'. It consists of three shallow pools formed into a reef with some spectacular hard coral formations and interesting marine life. Bedouin-style restaurants are located here for another relaxing and peaceful way to enjoy the shores. There are also plans to set up camps at the site to provide an extended diving and snorkelling haven.

Meet the locals

More than 350,000 people, many of whom are of Bedouin ancestry, call the Sinai peninsula home. It's a harsh and unforgiving environment, especially in the north where most choose to congregate. There are 14 distinct tribes, all with ties across the Middle East to families in the Negev, Jordan and Saudi Arabia.

The largest Bedouin tribe in the Sinai is the Sukwarka, whose centre is Al-Arish on the Mediterranean coast. So while it makes up a large proportion of the Bedouin population, you will probably have the least contact with this tribe's members if you are sticking to the Red Sea. Other important tribes scattered throughout the north and centre of the peninsula are the Tarabin, the Tyaha and the Haweitat.

The seven tribes in the south are collectively known as the Manzana or the Towara, 'Arabs of Al-Tor'. Members of these tribes work as guides for tourists wishing to travel into the Sinai interior, and hiring a Bedouin tour guide is actually quite easy. There are locations in most Red Sea resort communities where they gather collectively waiting for trade. Choosing a Bedouin guide not only ensures that you will be getting the best possible guide for your safari, but you will also be helping the Bedouin community, who rely on the income.

Bridging the cultural gap An invitation from a Bedouin guide or family should be treasured. Bedouin have fascinating traditions and a highly

Bedouin-style restaurants, Dahab

developed understanding of the environment. While the food at a banquet may not be to your particular taste you will cherish the memories of your experience.

Windsurfing

The windsurfing centres at Laguna Bay offer courses as well as daily rentals and include the Hilton, Coralia and Swiss Inn hotels.

Yoga

Whether it's ashtanga, hatha or kundalini, yoga is becoming increasingly popular in Dahab. The combination of sun, sea and a laid-back environment are all conducive to its practice. Yoga on nearby Mount Sinai is a regular draw, as are full-moon retreats into the nearby desert, taking advantage of all that silence and space. For more information, contact t 065 364 11 95

TAKING A BREAK

Al Capone ££ ❶ Why this fish restaurant is named after a Chicago gangster is a mystery. Perhaps, though, if the mobster could choose anywhere for an escape, it might be this place, where all the things on the menu are sold by weight. The staff encourage patrons to spend as long as they like – you can even get up from your table in the middle of a meal for a swim in the Gulf of Aqaba. ⓐ Masbat waterfront ⓣ 010 372 22 20 ⓦ www.dahabalcapone.com ❗ Cash only

Aladdin Tent ££ ❷ For an evening's taste of Bedouin life head for this eatery with its large lounge area and beach bar. There are regular shows with authentic Egyptian folkloric dances to music, and food is genuine Bedouin fare. ⓐ Happy Life Village, Wadi Qunal ⓣ 010 668 98 93 ⓦ www.happylifehotel.com ⓔ info@happylifehotel.com

Ali Baba ££ ❸ This atmospheric restaurant serves a wide choice of salads and dishes made entirely of fresh produce. Vegetarians are well catered for and for meat-eaters there are steaks, chicken and a daily barbecue. ⓐ Mashraba ⓣ 010 192 91 70 ⓦ www.alibaba-dahab.com ⓔ info@alibaba-dahab.com

Bedouin Lodge ££ ❹ Have dinner by candlelight in a Bedouin-like setting. Chilled-out atmosphere in an ideal shaded spot away from cold Dahab breezes. Very popular spot to have a few beers or some wine. ⓐ Masbat ⓣ 069 364 03 17 ⓦ www.Bedouin-lodge-dahab.com

Blue Beach Restaurant ££ ❺ Located at the Blue Beach Hotel with an extensive menu. Enjoy a tender steak cooked to your taste. The restaurant is inside and provides warm shelter in the winter and a cool environment in the hot summer months. ⓐ Asilah ⓣ 069 364 04 11

Dai Pescatori ££ ❻ At Sheikh Salem House, north of the Eel Garden site, experience good Italian food, especially the mixed appetisers, and the *semi-freddo* dessert. Enjoy the ravioli filled with shrimps! ⓐ Asilah ⓣ 012 797 23 61 ❗ Cash only

Funny Mummy ££ ❼ Very popular large restaurant of the New Sphinx Hotel directly on the beach. Lounge on the cushions under the atmospheric lighting and enjoy a vast array of great food. Water spray guns are provided to keep the pesky cats away. ⓐ Mashraba ⓣ 010 548 87 08

Jasmine Pension ££ ❽ Located right on the seafront with a suntrap of a veranda overhead. Varied menu with great breakfasts. It's an ideal place not only to eat, but also to hang out on brightly coloured cushions, relax, meet friends and enjoy the music. Water spray guns are provided to keep cats at bay. ⓐ Mashraba ⓣ 069 364 08 52 ❗ Cash only

The Kitchen ££ ❾ New, top-notch three-storey Indian, Thai and Chinese restaurant on the boulevard, next to the big supermarket. Lovely views of the sea, as well as food that you would associate with five-star restaurants of the countries themselves – you won't find fault with the delightful flavours. The restaurant doesn't serve alcohol, but you can buy your own in the off-licence next door and drink it without a corkage fee being charged. Also does takeaway and delivery. ⓐ Masbat ⓣ 019 595 97 64 ⓦ www.thekitchendahab.com

Leila's Bakery ££ ❿ Supplies all of Dahab with its freshly baked bread and pastries. Serves a great breakfast, lunch and dinner in a garden setting. Choose from a selection of traditional German snacks such as pretzels and apple strudel, or experience freshly cooked Egyptian cuisine. Indulge in their delicious brownies and cheesecake. ⓐ Sharia el-Fanar, Asilah ⓣ 010 693 56 69 ⓦ www.leilasbakery.com ❗ Cash only

Sea Bride ££ ⓫ This restaurant serves only seafood, but it's one of the best in Dahab for fish. ⓐ Masbat, away from the seafront ⓣ 069 364 08 91 ❗ Cash only

AFTER DARK

Unlike other Red Sea resorts, Dahab isn't known for its nightlife. Things stay pretty quiet after dark in these parts – and for this reason many travellers want to visit.

If you're looking for a drink and a dance, the following are worth checking out:

Furry Cup ⓬ This is the hotspot where Dahab's diving instructors come to mix and mingle. It's also a great place to pick up advice on which dive centres are better than others. A lively atmosphere is guaranteed almost every day of the week and the music is always good. ⓐ Blue Beach Club, Asilah ⓣ 069 364 04 11

Nesima Roof Lounge Bar ⓭ An outdoor elevated modern lounge bar that is the perfect setting for a sundowner. Happy hour from 19.00 to 21.00 every evening. ⓐ Mashraba ⓣ 069 364 03 20

Rush Lounge Bar ⓮ For a taste of pumping tunes, bongos and dancing, check out Rush on Wednesday and Friday nights. A real Balearic open-air feel, with a large iron dream-catcher gate, which acts as its entrance. Located up a small alley between the bridge and the now-defunct Tota restaurant ship. Set in a palm tree garden with a swimming pool, there's a party with DJs every Friday night. ⓐ Masbat ⓣ 069 364 18 67

The Treehouse ⓯ Popular club that has three big party nights a week: Tuesday, Wednesday and Saturday. Resident DJs play house and R&B music until 03.00. You can watch football championships on their big flat-screen TV or play some pool. ⓐ Mashraba ⓣ 069 364 09 47

Yalla Bar ⓰ Relax to chillout music on the beach or enjoy private parties on its wooden terrace with amazing views. Happy hour from 18.00 to 20.00. ⓐ Masbat by the lighthouse reef ⓣ 012 710 80 67 ⓦ www.yallabar.com

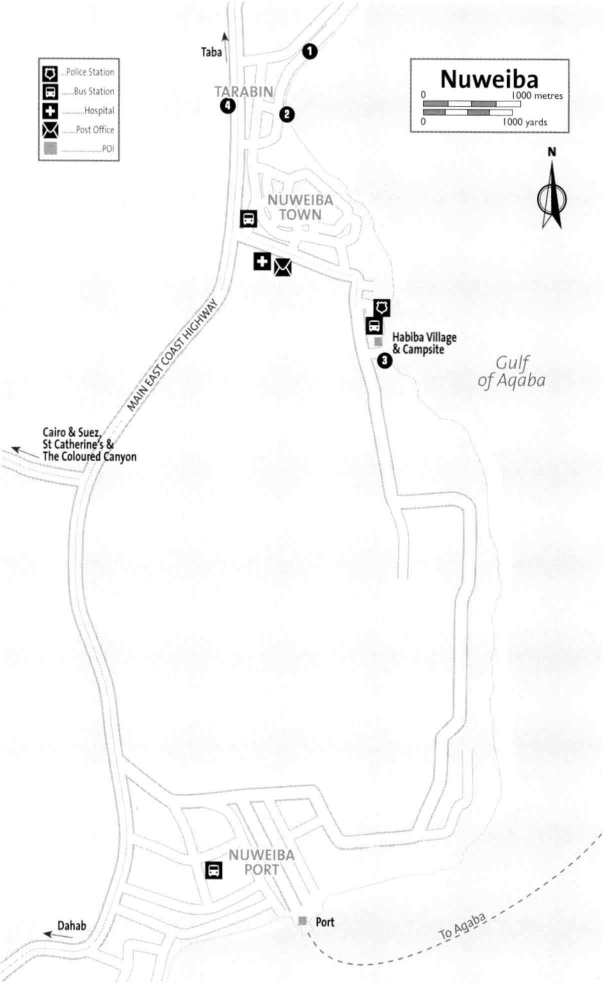
Nuweiba
0
1000 metres
0
1000 yards
N
...Police Station
.......Bus Station
............Hospital
........Post Office
..........................POI
Taba
TARABIN
NUWEIBA TOWN
MAIN EAST COAST HIGHWAY
Habiba Village & Campsite
Gulf of Aqaba
Cairo & Suez, St Catherine's & The Coloured Canyon
NUWEIBA PORT
Port
Dahab
To Aqaba

Nuweiba

Nuweiba benefits from a spectacular setting right on the coast of the Gulf of Aqaba. With its rugged mountains and sandy beaches, it is a less developed resort and offers a holiday experience off the beaten track. It is well worth visiting, especially as it is probably one of the cheapest places for a holiday anywhere in the country.

Before the Palestinian *intifada* of September 2000, Israelis constituted the bulk of visitors to this prime stretch of real estate. After this time, Israelis abandoned the area and the tourism industry all but died. The Iraq war hasn't helped either, resulting in low occupancy rates and a guaranteed warm welcome wherever you go in town.

Resorts are strung out over a long distance, thanks to a lack of town planning. There is no real centre to Nuweiba and many developments have been left half complete following the collapse of local businesses. The resorts that remain are of a high quality and incredibly affordable. It's a great place to mix and mingle with the local people and with travellers moving onwards to the Israeli border. A popular excursion is to Aqaba, Jordan's southernmost town. Visas are available on board the ferry.

ORIENTATION

Nuweiba is divided into three sections. To the south is the bus station, port, banks and the massive Hilton Coral Resort. **Nuweiba Town**, 8 km (5 miles) north, is a spread-out settlement of tourist shops, bazaars, hotels and cheap eateries. As more hotels have been constructed, the gap between Nuweiba Town and the port has diminished.

Further north is **Tarabin**. This neighbourhood is named after the local Bedouin tribe for which it is home. It is dominated by its stretch of beach, which is filled with small hotels and lined with bamboo-and-concrete huts. Less tranquil than it used to be, it caters predominantly to a travelling crowd looking to shun the big resorts of the area or stopping off en route to the Israeli border.

THINGS TO SEE & DO

Camel & jeep treks

After St Catherine's (see page 84), Nuweiba is probably the best location from which to organise a trip to see the Sinai peninsula. Local Bedouin guides offer a wide range of camel or jeep safaris from town with itineraries that feature a number of key destinations.

Durations depend on your chosen itinerary and mode of transport. Camels may feel more authentic, but they will also take two to three times longer than a jeep, and their usual swaying gait takes some getting used to.

Guides & destinations Prices for guides per day can vary quite considerably, with camel journeys priced at the high end of the scale. This price should include meals and the cost of registering the trip with the police. Drinking water may or may not be included. Make sure you check before you go as the further you travel away from 'civilisation', the more expensive it will be to replenish.

Choose your guide or tour operator carefully. You can book a package from any hotel, camp and supermarket in Tarabin. Your best bet will probably be a local Bedouin guide. Not only are they marginalised by local tour operators, they also know the region far better than anyone else.

There are dozens of places a safari can go, with the more popular destinations listed on the following pages. For detailed descriptions of some of the major sites, see page 78.

Camping

Nuweiba is popular for camping. There are dozens of secure campsites where you can pitch a tent, enjoy Bedouin meals and sit under the stars, lulled by the sound of the waves. If you don't have a tent, there are huts that you can rent out. **Habiba Camp** (t 012 217 66 24), which is situated close to Nuweiba City, is recommended. Check in advance that it isn't a day when they are expecting tour groups from Sharm if you want peace and relaxation.

Coloured Canyon

The Coloured Canyon lies between St Catherine's and Nuweiba, and derives its name from the layers of bright, multicoloured stones that resemble paintings on its steep, narrow walls. You will see shades of pink, orange and yellow in the rockface as you follow its winding path. It is quite sheltered from the wind, which makes it eerily silent – except when the large tour groups descend. It's a popular day trip from Sinai's resorts, so it is worth making an effort to arrive early in the day or late in the afternoon when the masses aren't there. Changes to this policy of 'come one, come all' are in motion. As the canyon falls under the boundaries of the Taba Protectorate, there are discussions under way to control crowds through payment of an entrance fee and implementation of daily number limits.

Diving & watersports

Nuweiba is not as focused on diving as the other Sinai resorts. There are still underwater areas worth exploring, many of them tailor-made for beginners. Shallow reefs offshore, such as the Stone House beyond the southern promontory, are perfect for snorkellers. Divers tend to head out to Ras Abu Gallum on day trips. Dives can be arranged through any of the four dive centres in Nuweiba.

Horse riding

It's possible to rent horses by the hour at the upmarket beach resort of Bawaki, located approximately 20 km (12 miles) up the coast from Tarabin. Rentals are reasonably cheap.

Meditation centre

Allow yourself to experience the power and beauty of the mountainous desert landscape by being in spiritual harmony with its elements. The Bedouin guide from El Khan Camp has a meditation centre in Ain Um Ahmed, the biggest oasis in South Sinai. The centre consists of tents and communal bathroom facilities for groups upon request. t 010 104 95 91 e anis@Sinai4you.com

Excursions

Ain al-Furtega A pleasing palm oasis located only 16 km (10 miles) from Nuweiba and easily accessible in a day. Its proximity to Nuweiba means it is usually the first port of call for any trekkers.

Ain Um Ahmed The largest oasis in the eastern Sinai. Ain Um Ahmed is known for its abundant palm trees, Bedouin community and stream. The stream becomes an icy torrent in the winter months when it is fed by the snow on the highest peaks of the Sinai.

Gebel Barga If you are a climber, then Gebel Barga should be a must. The climb is difficult (and therefore recommended only for those with at least some experience), but the stunning views over the eastern Sinai make the trek worthwhile. This trip is further away from other destinations. Budgeting two to three days for the return journey is recommended.

Mayat el-Wishwashi Once the largest rainwater cistern in the Sinai, Mayat has been reduced to a trickle. Go after the annual floods, when the water level rises and there is much more to look at.

Mayat Malkha Surrounded by colourful sandstone, Mayat Malkha is a palm grove fed by the waters of Mayat el-Wishwashi, which is much more lush during the flood season.

Wadi Sheikh Atiya This peaceful spot is the final resting place of the father of the Tarabin tribe, the largest Bedouin tribe in this region. There is a small oasis here and it is a popular destination for Bedouin pilgrimages.

TAKING A BREAK

Castle Beach £ ❶ Peaceful atmosphere and a popular meeting arena for travellers. It has a traditional oriental menu with a Bedouin slant, and fresh seafood. A friendly restaurant with good food. ⓐ Ras shaytan ⓣ 012 739 84 95

Cleopatra Restaurant ££ ❷ Good fish dishes and Egyptian meze are served at this establishment located opposite the Nuweiba Village Hotel. Basic, but filling. ⓐ Tarabin ⓣ 069 350 05 03 ❗ Cash only

Han Kang ££ ❸ Surprisingly good Chinese–Korean eatery opposite the Habiba Village. Basic 'oriental' cuisine is available alongside more intricate dishes. ⓐ Nuweiba Town ⓣ 069 350 09 70 ❗ Cash only

Castle Zaman £££ ❹ Located on the Al-Borqa Mountain, this impressive monument commands a dramatic view of four countries: Israel, Jordan, Saudi Arabia and Egypt. Incredible rustic setting for its restaurant, which specialises in the 'slow food' preparation of meat, fish and seafood. Ideal for a day excursion to take advantage of the infinity pool and bar. An underground dungeon-like tunnel leads to a treasure room full of Egyptian handicrafts. ⓐ Taba–Nuweiba Road ⓣ 018 214 05 91 ⓦ www.castlezaman.com

The Coloured Canyon between St Catherine's and Nuweiba

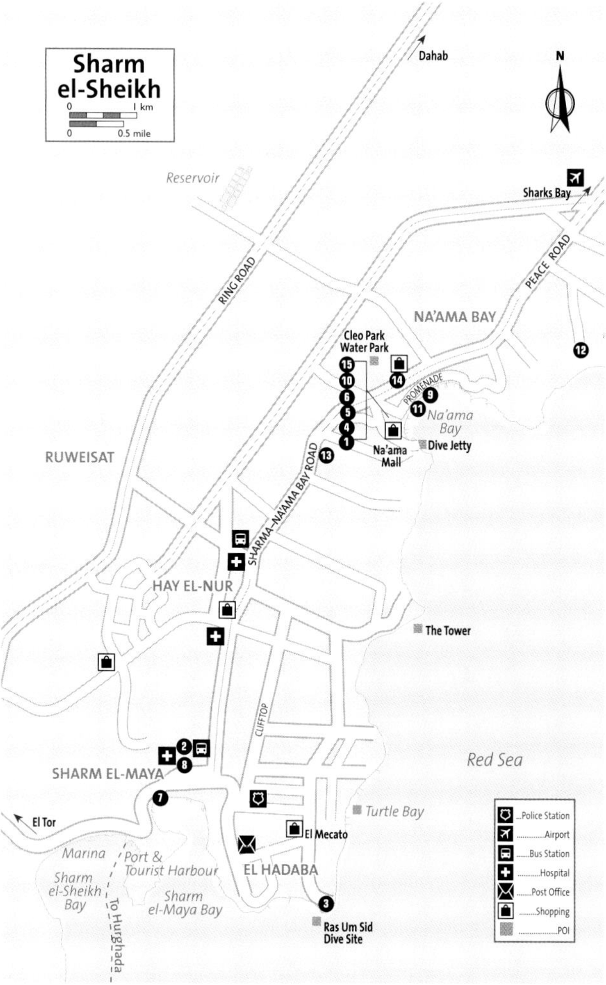
Sharm el-Sheikh
0 1 km
0 0.5 mile
N
Dahab
Reservoir
Sharks Bay
RING ROAD
PEACE ROAD
NA'AMA BAY
Cleo Park Water Park
PROMENADE
Na'ama Bay
Dive Jetty
Na'ama Mall
RUWEISAT
SHARMA–NA'AMA BAY ROAD
HAY EL-NUR
The Tower
CLIFFTOP
SHARM EL-MAYA
Red Sea
Turtle Bay
El Tor
El Mecato
Marina
Port & Tourist Harbour
EL HADABA
Sharm el-Sheikh Bay
Sharm el-Maya Bay
To Hurghada
Ras Um Sid Dive Site
...Police Station
...Airport
...Bus Station
...Hospital
...Post Office
...Shopping
...POI

Sharm el-Sheikh

The resort town of Sharm el-Sheikh didn't really exist until it was created by the Israelis in 1967 after they captured the Sinai in the Six Day War. Built to break the Egyptian blockade of the Tiran strait, the town developed slowly until divers 'discovered' the wealth of reefs located just offshore in the late 1970s. It was in Sharm el-Sheikh that Egypt's long-time president Mubarak resigned in February 2011.

Today, Sharm is one of Egypt's biggest tourist hotspots. The resort is actually a collection of areas, including the high-end luxury hotels north of Na'ama Bay, Na'ama Bay itself and the more workaday downtown core of Sharm el-Maya. Diving remains one of the biggest draws of the area, and there are plenty of operators who offer packages for both beginners and advanced. Holidaymakers are advised to stick to private hotel beaches in order to avoid attracting unwanted attention.

ORIENTATION

Sharm el-Sheikh consists of three main areas, the old market town of Sharm el-Maya and its bay; a number of other bays, where most of the tourist facilities are located; and the administrative area of El Hadaba, where there are holiday villas, apartments, condominiums and a few hotels. Sharm el-Sheikh's bays include, from south to north, Sharm el-Maya, Na'ama Bay, Garden Bay, Tiger Bay, Sharks Bay and Nabq Bay. Na'ama Bay is the most famous and developed of them all, with Sharks Bay following up the lead. However, there is currently a lot of interest in further developing Nabq Bay, a previously quiet area with good views of Tiran Island, as more malls, restaurants and bars start to appear. You can take a trip out to Tiran Island or quad bike into the mangroves, stopping for a swim and snorkel on the way into the desert.

Na'ama Bay

The major resort community of Na'ama Bay is located 7 km (4 miles) up the coast. Most of the five-star resorts and nightlife are located here. The sandy beaches are wide and well tended in Na'ama and the feeling is much more like a Mediterranean resort. You should feel comfortable wearing beachwear in all corners of this glamour spot; however, you should still avoid wearing bathing costumes away from the beach or pool, although this advice is ignored by many.

Ras Um Sid/El Hadaba

Southeast of Sharm el-Maya is the extremely built-up area of Ras Um Sid and El Hadaba. Here there's a huge shopping complex called El Mecato, many new hotels, houses and amusement parks. The area stretches from the Ras Um Sid dive site in the south to The Tower dive site. Resorts in this region vary in quality, with the high-end properties close to the beach.

Adjacent to downtown Sharm el-Maya is a cliffside area called Hadaba. There are many things here to keep visitors occupied. A residential neighbourhood, known as Hay el-Nur, lies further north and is designed for the middle classes. Here is where you will find the bus station, hospital and a well-stocked supermarket.

Sharm el-Maya

Sharm el-Maya is Sharm el-Sheikh's commercial core and home to the large market area, port and marina. If you're on a budget, then this is the part of town to explore if you're looking for a place to rest your head. As some of the neighbourhood is traditionally Egyptian in feel, modest clothing is advised when exploring the area.

THINGS TO SEE & DO

Please note that for some excursions outside Sharm el-Sheikh passports may be required.

Cleo Park Water Park

A fun place for kids, and a great way to entertain the family on a hot summer's day. Packed full of water slides and games for children and infants, attractions include a twister, multi-slide, space boat and more. The ground gets hot so take flip-flops. ⓐ Na'ama Bay ⓣ 069 360 44 00

Diving

Dive centres are two a penny in Sharm el-Sheikh, and especially in Na'ama Bay. An extensive range of courses, trips and equipment is available. Due to the stiff competition, all of the centres are generally recommended. Prices and operating styles do vary so it is worth shopping around for the best deals.

Those new to diving should try an introductory dive before committing to full lessons. Expect to pay £40–50 (US$60–80) including equipment.

If you get the bug, a five-day, open-water diving course is the next step. Any good course must include classroom theory. This will then lead to dives in a hotel swimming pool or just offshore followed by a couple of boat dives at the end. One of the most affordable and respected open-water PADI courses is offered by **Oonas Dive Club**. t 069 360 05 81 w www.oonasdiveclub.com

The beachfront at Sharm el-Sheikh

SHOPPING

Shopping in Sharm is possible in a number of modern malls and faux 'souks' designed to look like markets of yesteryear. If the thermometer is rising, the shopping malls are a good place to revive as almost all of them are air-conditioned.

Little in Sharm can't be found somewhere else in the country, and what you can find will invariably cost double what you would spend in Cairo or Luxor.

Some of the more interesting shops to check out include **Aladdin** at the Camel Hotel for arts and crafts; **Sharazaad** in Na'ama Bay Mall for scarfs, antiques, glass lamps and jewellery; and **Fenton Egyptian Handicrafts** in Tiran Mall, old market.

More advanced divers are also spoilt for choice. Almost all of the dive clubs and centres have courses that will train you to become an instructor, or offer specialised skills such as underwater navigation and night diving. Prices may vary significantly depending on the type of course, demand and time of year.

If you are already PADI certified and want to do a lot of boat diving, dive packages or liveaboards are probably the best option. A five-day dive package, including two dives per day, will cost from around £210.

Liveaboards offer more options and will take avid divers to places other boats just can't reach. Average costs are approximately £60 per person, per day for a boat of four to six air-conditioned cabins, including full board, airport transfers, tanks and weights. Diving equipment and alcohol will be extra.

For a full list of qualified diving operators in the Sharm area, contact the **South Sinai Association for Diving** on ⓣ 069 366 04 18 and see ⓦ www.southsinai.org

When in doubt as to whom to dive with, one of the best sources of information is other divers. If you haven't booked your dive prior to arriving at the resort, ask around at any of the local drinking dens.

Chances are you will run into a few opinionated souls. True divers will speak their mind as to which centres follow the best environmental policies as they are just as eager as you are to see the reefs thrive.

There is an amazing selection of dive spots in the region, which act as the major attraction for holidaymakers to this popular resort:

The striking lionfish is one of the species you may encounter when diving

Amphoras This diving point gets its name from a cargo of clay jars found on an Ottoman ship that sank on this reef. Luckily, the jars remain sealed as they contain mercury. This is an easy dive and can be negotiated by those new to undersea diving.

Paradise Paradise is a 20-minute sail north of Sharm. This dive site is visually spectacular and filled with vibrant colour and is a good place to spot sea turtles as they search for food.

Pinky's Wall Exactly halfway between Sharm and Na'ama Bay, Pinky's Wall is a wall that plunges into the blue depths of the sea. The reef is broken by vertical cracks and crevices. This is a classic wall dive as the coral wall drops away as far as the eye can see right from the surface.

Ras Um Sid This location is composed almost entirely of coral reef. However, Sharm's booming resort construction has caused some pollution to this stretch of waterfront.

The *Thistlegorm* Southeast of Sha'ab Mahmud, three and a half hours from Sharm el-Sheikh, lies one of the most famous wreck dive sites. The ship met her end thanks to German bomber planes in 1941 and lay undisturbed until Jacques Cousteau, the famous French diver, located her in 1956. Amid her depths, he found a living museum of World War II memorabilia, such as a full consignment of weaponry, Bedford trucks, Morris cars and BSA 350 motorbikes. The two railway locomotives she had been carrying had landed upright on the seabed on either side of the wreck. The *Thistlegorm* is best dived overnight and encompasses two dives; the first does a perimeter sweep of the boat and the second explores the wreck's interior.

The Tower A pleasant diving beach headlined by the Tower hotel. A coral pillar located just offshore drops 60 m (197 ft) into the sea depths and draws a mass of experienced divers.

The beautiful coastline at Sharm el-Sheikh

Turtle Bay Less of a diving spot than a gentle location for a snorkel and swim. The bay gets its name from green turtles that used to populate the area. Sadly, few of the creatures can be spotted today.

Sharks Bay

Located 10 km (6 miles) up the coast from Na'ama is Sharks Bay. Once a secluded getaway from the hustle and bustle of Sharm, the location

REEF PROTECTION

The development of large resorts on the Red Sea coastline may be beneficial to tourists in terms of offering them more selection, but they also have an impact on the environment. The coral reefs that originally attracted travellers to the region are threatened – but there are plenty of things you can do to ensure that the glorious reefs can be visited by generations to come.

Keep it clean Almost the entire Egyptian coastline is now a government protectorate, as is the Red Sea coast from Hurghada south to Sudan. What this means is that you can be penalised if you violate any part of the code of ethics determined by the government as necessary to keep the reef safe from harm. These code laws include:

- Do not collect, remove or damage any material, living or dead (including coral, fish and plants).
- Do not stir up sand as it is difficult for coral to remove sand particles and may result in stunted growth over a long period.
- Do not litter – especially cigarette butts.
- Do not fish or spearfish. If you see others doing it, report them to the Egyptian National Parks Office.
- Do not walk or anchor on any reef area. Try to time snorkelling with the high tide so you can swim – and not walk – over the living reef.
- Do not feed the fish as this disturbs the reef's ecological balance.
- Do not touch, kneel on or kick coral as this will cause permanent, irreversible damage.

Cause and effect Killing the coral will eventually kill off the fish. If you attempt to skirt the laws by breaking off coral to bring home as a souvenir, you may be prosecuted. Please do not attempt to pay *baksheesh* (a tip) to the dive centre as it is illegal. Do not be tempted to flout these rules just because you know you can get around them. It doesn't help anyone involved. The main rule to follow above all others is: leave the reef how you found it.

Unwritten rules While they aren't official, there are other tips you can follow to make your diving experience have less of an impact on the environment:

- Practise maintaining proper buoyancy control. This fact is touched on very little during beginners' open-water courses, yet most of the major damage done to reefs occurs when divers descend too fast and collide with the reef. Please remember that because the Red Sea is extremely saline, you will need extra weight to overcome the heightened buoyancy.
- Take care in underwater caves. There are plenty of such caves to explore in the Red Sea; however, long periods of time spent inside them may result in your air bubbles rising up and forming pockets of gas within the roof.
- Be conscious of your fins. Avoid contact with reefs and try not to kick up too much sand.
- Do not wear gloves. Gloves are banned in Ras Mohamed National Park, but many dive centres are lax in enforcing the rule.

is now packed with large holiday villages. A sandy track was once the only way you could reach the area, but today a series of tarmacked roads is used to service the hotels and to shuttle holidaymakers back and forth to Na'ama or the airport.

Despite the name, Sharks Bay rarely sees any sharks, although there was a fatal attack in 2010 in which five people died in nearby Na'ama Bay. Instead, the waters here are home to a lovely selection of tropical fish attracted by the coral gardens just offshore. Visitors from other resorts have to pay a charge to use the beach. This fee includes the use of the showers and one soft drink.

TAKING A BREAK

Andrea's £ ❶ Cheap chicken dishes and quality Egyptian yummies. Good value makes this a great place for those on a budget.
ⓐ Off Sharma–Na'ama Bay Road, next to the Hard Rock Cafe
ⓘ Cash only

El Masrian £ ❷ Quick and easy *fuul* and *ta'amiya* (see page 96) takeaway in the heart of the market. Great for a fast lunch or late-evening bite. ⓐ Sharm el-Maya market ⓣ 069 366 29 04 ⓘ Cash only

The area of Al Faraana Reef in Sharm el-Sheikh

Al-Fanar ££ ❸ The place to go for a romantic meal, Al-Fanar boasts a beautiful waterfront location at the base of a lighthouse. Italian meals are served Bedouin-style under the stars. Go for the views more than the food. ⓐ Ras Um Sid ⓣ 069 366 22 18

Far East Restaurants ££ ❹ A choice of Chinese, Thai, Indian and sushi all under one roof on the first floor overlooking the main strip. Will deliver too. ⓐ On the corner of Sharma–Na'ama Bay Road ⓣ 069 360 34 18 ⓦ www.dragon-group.org

Hard Rock Cafe ££ ❺ Sharm's most popular nightspot is a branch of the well-known chain dedicated to the world of rock music. Expect typical hamburgers at an atypical price. A good children's menu attracts those travelling with tots during the day while the 20- and 30-somethings patrol at night. ⓐ Off Sharma–Na'ama Bay Road ⓣ 069 360 26 65

Pomodoro ££ ❻ You will need to book ahead as it tends to get really busy. Italian meat and fish dishes are its speciality, as well as home-made pizza, salads and vegetarian dishes. Has seating indoors and outside. Great buzz, but don't expect a peaceful atmosphere as it is on the main strip of Na'ama Bay. ⓐ Na'ama Bay ⓣ 069 360 07 00

Safsafa Restaurant ££ ❼ Probably the best-loved restaurant in town, the Safsafa is celebrated for its seafood. Family-run and extremely small, this eatery only has eight tables which are full at all hours. Recommended dishes include calamari and *babaghanoug* (see page 97). ⓐ Sharm el-Maya ⓣ 069 366 04 74 ❗ No alcohol. Cash only

Sinai Star ££ ❽ This popular seafood restaurant is especially well liked by tour groups. Fish dishes are particularly recommended. Beer and wine are not available on the menu, but if you ask nicely, they will get a waiter to run to a nearby shop to pick up a few bottles for you. ⓐ Sharm el-Maya ⓣ 069 366 03 23 ❗ Cash only

Tandoori ££ ❾ Pleasant Indian eatery in an outdoor courtyard location. There is a wide variety of tandoori dishes to choose from, but it's the dhal that will keep you coming back for more. ⓐ Camel Hotel, Promenade ⓣ 069 360 07 00

AFTER DARK

Bus Stop ❿ Sharm's hottest nightclub sees a wild crowd – especially on Thursday evenings. It's the centre of the action for fans of decadence and dancing till dawn. ⓐ Sanafir Hotel ⓣ 069 360 01 98 ⓦ www.sanafirhotel.com

Camel Dive Bar ⓫ The drinking spot of choice for serious divers. If you want to trade tips on sightings, equipment and reef quality, then this is where to come. ⓐ Adjoins the Camel Hotel ⓣ 069 360 07 00

La Folie Bar ⓬ Looking for a quiet drink? Then this is the place to go. Tables sit almost directly over the water, taking in views of the twinkling lights of Na'ama Bay. ⓐ Iberotel Lido ⓣ 069 360 26 03

Little Buddha ⓭ Typical of the chain, candlelit, Far Eastern décor, and good atmosphere. Dine, drink and dance the night away. ⓐ Tropitel, end of main strip ⓣ 069 360 10 30 ⓦ www.littlebuddha-sharm.com

Pirates Bar ⓮ This is another bar for dedicated divers. More geared towards long-term residents and locals, the place has a cheesy nautical theme. Often has discount promotions on drinks. ⓐ Hilton Fayrouz Hotel ⓣ 069 360 01 40

Rooftop Bar ⓯ Feel like a sultan as you recline on cushions sipping mint tea under the stars. ⓐ Sanafir Hotel ⓣ 069 360 01 98 ⓦ www.sanafirhotel.com

Taba

Since 1982, Taba has served as the main border crossing between Egypt and Israel. It has a lot to attract tourists to the area, and is still fairly unspoilt with some beautiful coastline to enjoy.

About 17 km (10½ miles) south of Taba, a new development of luxury hotels has been constructed in the ritzy location dubbed '**Taba Heights**' (ⓦ www.tabaheights.com). It houses a casino, shops, bars, restaurants, spas, a medical clinic, golf course and water park. It is also a significant dive area.

The five-star resorts have a similar scheme to Port Ghalib, whereby you are able to use the facilities of any hotel regardless of your hotel of residence.

Tourism development was initiated as a direct result of the 14-day free Sinai visa available coming from Israel; however, tourism was badly affected in October 2004, when 34 people were killed in a suicide truck bombing of the Taba Hilton lobby. Security is tight, but discreet.

THINGS TO SEE & DO

Pharaoh's Island

This delightful getaway is 7 km (4 miles) before the border and just 250 m (275 yds) off the coast. Dominated by the restored castle of Salah ad-Din, it is a pleasant place to spend half a day enjoying some nice snorkelling and sunbathing.

The fortress was built by the Crusaders in 1115, but captured and expanded by Saladin in 1170. At the height of the Crusades, it was considered a major defence post protecting the Muslim holy cities of Mecca and Medina. Some of the restoration jobs have been a bit haphazard, however, especially the bits where concrete has been used to shore up crumbling walls.

If it's snorkelling you're after, then you should head to the southern end of the island where the coral is good, or to the northeastern coast where the reefs are even better.

TAKING A BREAK

Petra Camp £ Petra Camp comes highly recommended, and it offers sumptuous Bedouin fare. It also serves a delicious barbecue dinner with nice salads and fresh juices. ⓐ Tarabeen ⓣ 069 350 00 86

CROSSING THE BORDER

The border with Israel is open 24 hours a day, despite the ongoing Palestinian and Egypt–Israel political issues. The only exceptions are Yom Kippur and Eid el-Adha. No traffic whatsoever passes between the two nations on these two important holy days. You should also avoid attempting to cross into Israel after mid-morning on Friday or all day Saturday when transport and businesses shut down for Shabbat.

Departing Egypt is a relatively quick and painless process. Israelis issue free three-month visas to all EU, US, Canadian, Australian and New Zealand citizens. Travellers must walk a no-man's-land between the Egyptian and Israeli checkpoints.

Coming from Israel, there is an exit tax payable to Israeli authorities and an entry tax payable to the Egyptian government, which is required of all travellers leaving Israel. Visas can be obtained in Tel Aviv or same-day from the Eilat consulate.

If you are just planning to travel within the Sinai peninsula, consider obtaining a 14-day, Sinai-only visa, which is issued free at the border. Once across the border you may be approached by taxi drivers who try to convince you that the distance to the bus that takes passengers on to the coast towns of Nuweiba and Sharm is too far to walk. Do not listen to them. Even if you have a lot of luggage, it's really just a five-minute stroll away. If you need Egyptian pounds, wait until you get into Egypt, where the exchange rate is better.

Visitors have been able to enter the Gaza Strip from Egypt with effect from May 2011.

Ancient Egyptian mural

EXCURSIONS
Out & about

From Hurghada

Mons Porphyrites

Located 40 km (25 miles) into the desert, on a side track off the main coast road 20 km (12 miles) north of Hurghada, is an ancient porphyry quarry known as Mons Porphyrites. Originally worked by the Romans, the mine produces a precious white-and-purple crystalline stone that was mined for use in sarcophagi, columns and decorative work. Much valued by Rome's imperial family, the mines had encampments, workshops and temples built specifically for the workers and engineers.

In order to transport the stone from the mine, blocks were dragged 150 km (93 miles) to the Nile, where they were then shipped to such locales as Baalbek and Constantinople. Lying around the quarries is a ruined town with two large cisterns and an unfinished Ionic temple. To get the most out of the visit, a guide is recommended. A large number of tours from Hurghada visit the area, making the town seem extremely crowded at certain times of the day – try to go off-peak (late afternoon).

Mons Claudianus

Less historically important and more remote is Mons Claudianus. Also a Roman mining centre, Mons Claudianus was known for its output of black-flecked granite. Some of the stone produced here was used to construct the Parthenon and Trajan's Forum in Rome.

Only the most hardened of Roman prisoners were shipped to this desolate spot to work as forced labour, as it was considered to be an 'end of the line' destination. Guards fared little better – a spell here was considered a hardship post for soldiers of ill repute. The remains of the tiny cells they inhabited still exist, in addition to an immense cracked pillar, left where it fell 2,000 years ago.

A guide with a vehicle suitable for the rough terrain and experience of guiding in remote desert locations is required for this trip. You can usually arrange this through your hotel.

St Paul's Monastery

Zafarana

Far from Hurghada, yet well worth the trip, is the town of Zafarana. Gateway to the monasteries of St Anthony and St Paul, the town is an important centre for Coptic Christians.

St Anthony is a fortified religious community hidden in the barren cliffs of the Eastern Desert. Built in the 4th century AD, the site is located at the foot of Gebel al-Galala al-Qibliya – a location specifically chosen in order to help guard it against almost constant attacks from Bedouin and Muslims from the 8th to the 15th centuries. At certain points in its bloody history, the monastery could only be entered using a large basket and wooden winch. Ask nicely and the current residents will show you how it works.

Zafarana is easy to reach using regular buses that ply the road between Suez and Hurghada. Budget for at least two days to undertake the return journey from Hurghada.

Church of St Anthony The oldest part of the monastery is the Church of St Anthony, built over St Anthony's tomb. It contains the largest collection of Coptic wall paintings in Egypt, all newly restored after extensive renovation. There are currently over sixty monks and five novices at St Anthony's, dedicating their lives to poverty, chastity, obedience and prayer. The monks have almost completed construction of a museum that will better showcase the monastery's collection of ancient manuscripts and crosses.

St Paul's Monastery St Paul's Monastery has always been overshadowed by St Anthony. Its founder was only 16 when he fled his hometown of Alexandria in order to escape the persecution of Emperor Decius. Following his death, St Paul's followers decided to build a monastery to honour him. Much smaller than St Anthony's, the complex is more primitive looking than its better-known neighbour. Monks will show you around the chapels and identify icons.

From Marsa Alam

Rock inscriptions & ancient mines

A plethora of rock inscriptions exist on the Marsa Alam–Edfu road, many dating back to prehistoric times. Hunting scenes with dogs chasing ostriches, giraffe depictions and hieroglyphs are just some of the drawings that can be spotted. You don't have to travel far outside the city limits to see drawings because the smooth grey rock of the area was perfect for carving. Police are nervous about foreigners travelling on roads, so a guide is recommended as much for your protection as to avoid police harassment.

Further afield are a number of ancient gold mines in the mountains south of town. Of particular interest are those at **Wadi Miya**, also known for the remains of a temple said to be built by Seti I.

Among the other sites worth considering are the caves and remains at **Wadi Hammamat**, **Wadi Mineh** and **Wadi Barramiyah**. Wadi Hammamat is celebrated for its beautiful hieroglyphs, Wadi Mineh for its wealth of petroglyphs and Wadi Barramiyah for its rock-cut Temple of Kanais. One of the best parts of any excursion into the desert is the actual drive. The landscape is wonderful and the road is almost empty except for the occasional grazing camel. Visitors can only reach these remote mines on foot or by camel with an experienced guide. Buses do run along the route, making drops at Wadi Hammamat from the coast road, but it is much easier to plan a visit as part of an organised tour. Another option is to hire a taxi for the day. Hiring a car and driver should be reasonably inexpensive.

For climatic reasons, trips to see the mines and inscriptions are recommended only from mid-September to mid-May. When setting out, ensure that you have enough water and fuel for your entire journey.

El Quseir

El Quseir is a major port located almost exactly halfway between Marsa Alam and Hurghada. The town has a long history dating back to Pharaonic times, when it was a major launching point for boats sailing to Punt.

El Quseir is a particularly pleasant town to wander through due to its sleepy charm and intriguing architecture. Old coral-block buildings with wooden balconies surround the waterfront interspersed by the domed tombs of saints – these were mostly pious pilgrims who died en route to or from Mecca.

Until the 10th century, El Quseir was a major exit point for pilgrims travelling to Mecca for the haj. While its importance dwindled over time, the town remained strategically key and was fortified by the Ottomans six centuries later. The British took over the town in the 19th century, beating the French for control. At one stage, it was the point of importation for all spices going to Britain from India. The opening of the Suez Canal in 1869 ended this period of prosperity, prompting a long period of decline.

The fortress The formidable fortress dominates the town, despite scars that remain from a heated battle between the British and occupying French forces in the 19th century when over 6,000 cannonballs rained down on the structure.

Restoration work on the fortress was completed some years ago, during which time a visitors' centre was built in order to display

Sunset over the Red Sea at El Quseir

collections discussing local history, Red Sea mining, local monasteries, important trade in the region and the history of the haj.

Across from the fortress is the 19th-century shrine of a Yemeni sheikh. His gravestone is located in a niche in the wall of the building.

Berenice

Founded by Ptolemy II, Berenice was an important trading post until the 5th century AD. Just up until a few years ago, it could only be visited with a special military permit but now it is developing into what will become the southernmost holiday destination on the Egyptian Red Sea coast. The coast itself is lined with mangrove swamps, unspoilt bays and coves still rich in historic sites.

Diving & snorkelling Join the dive boats for offshore snorkelling or stay on the beach and explore the 5 km (3 miles) of reefs. The peninsula of Ras Banas off Foul Bay is popular; however, strong currents can limit even the most experienced to certain places. Particularly attractive are the three remote islands of Daedalus, Rocky and Zabargad, and the two outer reef systems of Fury Shoal and St John Reef. Places such as the Qulan Islands, Sha'ab Makhsour, Sha'ab Ossama, Sattaya and Sha'ab Claude are reachable on day trips. You can organise dives through **Barakuda Diving Centre**. ⓣ 010 009 12 92 ⓦ www.barakuda-diving.com

The marine areas are protected by environmentally friendly organisations that cooperate to help conserve the underwater life in the region and perform regular checks to ensure the presence of mooring buoys at all dive sites.

Excursions A nearby point of interest is the ruins of the Temple of Semiramis, as well as the volcanic island of Zabargad, previously famous as the source of the semi-precious gem olivine, which is said to have spiritual powers. Peridot Hill offers spectacular views of the surrounding lagoons, which are rich in marine life and home to pods of dolphins. The **Fustat Wadi El Gemel Eco-lodge** in the national park offers desert safaris by jeep, quad bike or camel. ⓣ 010 123 15 15

From Sinai resorts

Coloured Canyon

Second only to St Catherine's as a day-trip destination, the Coloured Canyon derives its name from the layers of bright, multicoloured stones that resemble paintings on its steep, narrow walls. As the canyon is sheltered from the wind, it is extremely silent – a fact that contributes to its eerie atmosphere. Unfortunately, the sheer volume of visitors often means that you can't appreciate the calm as much as you might wish to.

The shades of colour that can be seen here range from white to yellow to vibrant red. They are particularly reminiscent of similar formations found at Petra in Jordan. Hikers will find that the colours are extremely well set off by the tiny strip of vivid blue sky above. At some points, the canyon is just 1.5 m (5 ft) wide.

Hikers entering the Coloured Canyon

A BRIEF HISTORY

Water erosion during the Quaternary Period provided the foundations on which the Coloured Canyon developed. A glance at the spectacular landscape of the region will take you through eras of geological history, as you can see the many layers of sandstone, limestone and rocks of marine origin that have been carved by the erosion over millions of years.

The narrowest and most impressive section of the canyon is about 700 m (765 yds) in length, and presents two passages that require considerable fitness to get through. After making your way through the section, you will find that the canyon widens a bit and enters a broad wadi. Keep to the right until you reach a rock cliff with a steep trail that will need to be climbed to return to the high land.

If you arrived here with a private driver, this makes a good location to arrange a pick up – otherwise, you'll have to walk all the way back along the 2.5-km (1½-mile) trail.

Gebel Musa

The climb up Gebel Musa (which translates as the 'Mountain of Moses'), believed to be the same as Mount Horub from the Bible, is an excursion not to be missed by any travellers who tour St Catherine's. The hike to the summit requires about three hours and can be made by two different routes, which converge along the final part of the hike. Sikket Saydna Musa ('The Path of Moses') is believed to follow the route taken by Moses when he first climbed the mount. It consists of a long, steep stairway of approximately 3,700 steps cut directly into the living rock by the monks.

Spring of Moses After about 30 minutes, walkers pass this spring, which gurgles out into a small grotto and runs past a chapel dedicated to the Virgin Mary.

Gate of Confession After the spring and chapel, one encounters the Gate of Confession, so called because a monk once heard confession here from pilgrims in ancient times, in order that they might accede to the sacred mountain cleansed of their sins.

Amphitheatre Halfway up the mountain, walkers reach a plain surrounded by granite known as the 'Amphitheatre of the Seventy Wise Men of Israel' – called this because the Seventy Wise Men who accompanied Moses on his climb stopped here, since only the prophet could present himself in the presence of God.

Chapel of the Holy Trinity The summit of the mountain offers breathtaking views. There is also a chapel dedicated to the Holy Trinity that was rebuilt in 1934 on the grounds of an existing church from the 4th century AD. Its interior decoration illustrates the life of Moses using colourful frescoes. Alongside the chapel is a mosque that supposedly lies just above the cave where Moses spent 40 days and the Lord appeared to the prophet Elijah.

Nabq Mangrove Forest

The region of Nabq, which extends over 600 sq km (232 sq miles), was declared a protected territory in 1992 and incorporated into the Ras Mohamed National Park. The delicate natural equilibrium of this coastal strip justifies the policy of extremely strict environmental protection that is implemented by park authorities. The forest is a place of great beauty, offering visitors the opportunity to observe a lagoon area teeming with life, in contrast to the silent void of the surrounding desert. The most numerous residents of the beaches are hermit and mud crabs. You'll see plenty of them scurrying on the sand.

Nabq holds the largest mangrove forest in the Sinai, extending along more than 4 km (2½ miles) of the shoreline. These plants, with their distinctive roots on the water's surface, filter seawater and expel salt crystals from the leaves. They also restrain sediments, thus limiting erosion on the entire coastline. A vast number of animal species call Nabq home.

HOW TO GET TO NABQ BY CAR
Once past the Ras Nasrani airport, follow the paved road that runs parallel to the coast through a built-up area of hotels and tourist villages. Be careful not to leave it, as part of it is surrounded by unmarked minefields. Continue on until you reach the checkpoint. At this point, rangers will charge you to enter the park. Access to the wadis surrounding Nabq is only permitted after issue of permits by the park management as they contain a wide variety of rock and mineral formations. ! Do carry your passport just in case you are asked to produce it

Birdwatchers will find the region of particular interest as numerous herons, ospreys and storks are drawn to the park in order to gorge themselves on the buffet of small fish that swim in the shallow waters surrounding the mangroves.

Oasis of Ain Um Ahmed

Ain Um Ahmed is one of the least visited and most beautiful oases in the Sinai. It is a huge palm grove broken here and there by small gardens and orchards cultivated by the few Bedouin families that live in a nearby village.

This is a place with abundant water, which springs forth pure and clear after travelling through long subterranean passages. The water is gathered by the Bedouin in cisterns partially concealed amid the palm trees.

Ras Mohamed

A national park since 1983, the peninsula of Ras Mohamed is located at the southern tip of the Sinai. It is an unspoilt site of remarkable beauty and exceptional interest in terms of nature and wildlife. The park has four goals that it strives to achieve:

- To provide information and education to visitors
- To explain the purposes of the park to the Bedouin, so that they can better manage their own land

A LUNAR LANDSCAPE

To best appreciate the Ain Um Ahmed oasis, look for a well-marked track near the Bedouin village that takes the same name as the oasis. It will climb to a narrow passageway between huge boulders that will then open up into a scenic point overlooking a broad expanse of powdery-looking white rocks. Depending on how the light hits them, colours can leap up ranging from light blue to ochre and deep red. Especially worth noticing is the majestic **Ras el-Qelb** mountain that stands approximately 1,000 m (3,300 ft) high. The track then becomes a true road that runs a number of metres wedged between the mountain and the deep multicoloured sandstone bed of a dry stream.

Walkers particularly enjoy this stretch of protected land as there are a number of well-marked routes ideal for exploration. If you do decide to take a stroll, carry plenty of water and embark either early in the morning or in the late afternoon as the sun can get extremely hot. You must also stick to the pathways as the surrounding land is protected. A few steps off any trail could cause damage to an extremely fragile ecosystem. Please follow these simple rules: no camping, no fires, no smoking, no alcohol and no interfering with the flora and fauna.

- To promote scientific research and environmental monitoring
- To ensure that laws designed to protect the natural heritage of the park are adhered to

Diving at Ras Mohamed Both the land and surrounding water are considered part of the park. There are some incredible diving spots located just offshore. One of the best ways to arrive at the park is by sea, as this allows visitors the opportunity to examine the magnificent seabeds. One of the best locations to see the interplay of the land and marine ecosystems is from an observation platform called the

'Shark Observatory' on the east side of Hidden Bay. If you can cope with the summer heat, this site is spectacular from mid-June to mid-August when the fish are mating, grouping together in large schools out in the deep water.

Saltwater lake at Ras Mohamed National Park

St Catherine's Monastery

The monastery of St Catherine is located at the foot of the Gebel Musa, at an elevation of 1,570 m (5,150 ft) above sea level. Founded by the Byzantine Emperor Justinian between AD 527 and 547, the complex boasts a fascinating history that can trace its roots back to the Bible.

According to the story of Moses, the tablets of the Ten Commandments were given to the Hebrews on the plain of El-Raha in the Sinai peninsula after 50 days of marching through the desert. Mount Horeb, which is located near the plain and has since been dubbed Gebel Musa (the 'Mountain of Moses'), became a place of pilgrimage and prayer for the earliest Christians and a small monastic community was born.

While tours of the monastery are on offer, most of the buildings are off-limits to visitors. Rather, it is the surrounding countryside and grounds that make a visit here an absolute must. If you would like to include a tour in your itinerary, plan your visit in the morning hours as guides are only permitted between 09.00 and 12.00. On Fridays, Sundays, major religious holidays and during periods of spiritual retirement there is restricted access to the monastery. Check with

St Catherine's Monastery, once a great Christian pilgrimage destination

THE LEGEND

Between the 8th and 9th centuries, the monks found the body of St Catherine, which, according to legend, had been transported by angels to the summit of Gebel Katherina. The saint's body was placed in a sarcophagus inside the basilica where it still lies. It was the Crusaders of the 11th century who spread the cult of St Catherine throughout Europe, making the monastery one of the great Christian pilgrimage destinations.

your tour operator or hotel prior to setting off. 069 347 00 32
09.00–12.00 daily (restrictions Fri & Sun)

Tiran

The island of Tiran is a diver's paradise. Enormously important in military terms, the island actually belongs to Saudi Arabia, yet is 'on loan' to Egypt. While you can't step foot on Tiran, the landmass is a wonderful location to visit as part of a day trip due to its enchanting diving opportunities.

Tiran is located at the centre of the strait of Tiran, which closes off the Gulf of Eilat and is bounded by the Sinai peninsula and the Saudi Arabian coast. The coral reefs off the southeastern coast of Tiran and to the northwest are considered to be the best preserved in the entire Sharm region.

Wadi el-Ain

The sandy Wadi el-Ain is dotted with acacias, palm trees and wells that are protected by barbed wire. It is a stunning location for a spot of contemplation and the perfect ending point after a peaceful hike.

If you plan on visiting, be sure to bring your passport as there is a military checkpoint just before you reach the oasis. Without identification, the armed forces won't let you past their gates. Your journey will be much quicker if you have a driver and/or guide with you to handle the translation and act as your 'agent'.

THE CORAL REEFS

Four coral reefs occupy the centre of the strait: Gordon Reef, Jackson Reef and two smaller reefs, Thomas Reef and Woodhouse Reef. All are favourite diving spots for experienced divers, yet you will find few who talk about it, preferring to keep this jewel of a location as untouched as possible. Gordon Reef offers intriguing views thanks to the remains of a wrecked freighter that ran aground on the reef's coral shallows. Almost every species of coral fish can be found close to the freighter's slowly deteriorating shell.

In these sites, the fauna is extremely abundant. Large fish and sharks are common due to the presence of powerful currents, which also promote the growth of alcyonarians and gorgonians covering the walls of the reef. Divers and snorkellers have been challenged by these currents and are advised to always explore with a partner and/or experienced guide. Trips are easily arranged from Na'ama Bay.

Wadi Magara

Fans of adventure will love taking an off-road trip to the Wadi Magara turquoise mines, which are reached by following an ancient track eastwards up Wadi Sidri from Abu Rudeis. The mines have been worked since as far back as the 1st Dynasty. As you walk deep into the valley, you may even notice small turquoises, though these are of little value. If you climb higher, you will come to carvings on the rock face depicting 4th- and 5th-Dynasty Pharaohs. Directly across the valley, on the hill opposite, are the remains of workshops, workers' houses and a fort – all Pharaonic.

Camel camping One of the most enjoyable ways to enjoy this region is to travel through it on a camel. Camels with guides can be hired to venture to the wadi from Dahab, Nuweiba, Sharm el-Sheikh and St Catherine's. Treks will usually take from one to ten days.

Be prepared to produce a medical certificate, and bring along your own sleeping bag and first-aid kit. You may also be required to register your trip with the police for security purposes.

King Sekhemkhet Back down on the sandy wadi floor, you can picnic beneath the shade of an acacia tree. Here, one can also see a celebrated bas-relief dating from the Old Kingdom, depicting King Sekhemkhet (3rd Dynasty, about 2600 BC), which was uncovered by a British explorer in 1868.

Mines & inscriptions tour The Wadi Magara is best visited as part of a tour. Most packages to the mines will also include visits to the larger mines of Serabit el Khadim, where there is also a 12th-Dynasty sanctuary dedicated to the god Hathor. They will also stop at Wadi Moqattab, otherwise known as the 'Valley of the Inscriptions'. Here you will find mostly Nabatean and Greek inscriptions, but also Coptic and Arabic texts dating from the 1st to the 6th centuries AD.

A camel ride is an Egyptian experience not to be missed!

Alexandria & Aswan

Alexandria

In Cleopatra's day, Alexandria was a glittering jewel of a city. Sadly, however, little remains of its glorious past. Until recently, few had reason to visit Egypt's most European of cities, but recent innovations have changed all of that as numerous efforts are being made to transform the fortunes of this once proud metropolis.

THINGS TO SEE & DO

Bibliotheca Alexandrina

This massive structure is Alexandria's most visible attempt to put the city back on the world's cultural map. Inspired by the original great library – one of the Seven Wonders of the Ancient World – the Bibliotheca is designed to hold eight million books in its vast space. Unfortunately, the library's budget has fallen short of expectations and only a few hundred thousand works call the Bibliotheca home. The most interesting aspect of the museum is a fascinating exhibit chronicling the history of the city through the use of drawings, maps

Local produce at the market

and early photographs. ⓐ El Shatby, Alexandria ⓦ www.bibalex.org ⓛ 11.00–19.00 Sat–Thur, 15.00–19.00 Fri ⓘ Admission charge

Catacombs of Kom Ash-Shuqqafa

Home to the largest Roman burial site in Egypt, the catacombs were discovered accidentally in 1900 when a donkey fell through the ground. They consist of three tiers of tombs and chambers cut into the rock to a depth of 35 m (115 ft). The catacombs are entered by descending a spiral staircase cut into a circular shaft. If you are nervous about tight, dark or enclosed spaces, you may want to give this sight a miss. ⓛ 09.00–17.00 daily

National Museum of Alexandria

Housed in a beautifully restored palace, the National Museum is home to nearly 2,000 archaeological pieces exhibited throughout the building. Each floor contains artefacts from prehistoric, Pharaonic, Graeco-Roman, Coptic and Islamic eras, and includes mummies and antiquities saved during the underwater excavations some years ago. ⓐ Fouad Street, Alexandria ⓛ 09.00–17.00 daily (till 16.00 in winter) ⓘ Admission charge

Aswan

Egypt's southernmost city is the gateway to Africa and home to the bulk of the country's Nubian population. It's a prosperous marketplace at the crossroads of ancient caravan roads, and a popular resort. The city is most often combined as a two-centre package with holidays in Marsa Alam.

THINGS TO SEE & DO

Abu Simbel

Located 280 km (174 miles) south of Aswan, Abu Simbel is one of Egypt's 'signature' sights and is most often visited as a day excursion using regular charter flights. Two temples stare out from the cliff face at Abu Simbel – built by Ramses II as a warning against troublesome Nubians.

Before the creation of Lake Nasser the temples overlooked a bend in the Nile River and dominated the landscape. They remain as impressive as ever and are well worth the financial investment required to visit.

Construction of the Aswan High Dam in the 1960s would have drowned the temples beneath Lake Nasser. Instead, a massive operation funded by UNESCO raised them to a new and higher site nearby.

08.00–17.00 daily

Kôm Ombo

The double Temple of Sobek and Horus, dating from the Ptolemaic period, enjoys a lovely setting on a low promontory overlooking the Nile. It's a bit of a long journey outside Aswan, often done on an overnight trip. One of the most enjoyable ways to arrive is to hire a felucca from Aswan and sail up the river, tying up beneath the temple to spend the night.

Philae

The temple of Philae was moved to its present site, the island of Agilqiyyah, in 1980 following flooding caused by the completion of the Aswan High Dam. Built over 2,000 years ago in honour of the goddess Isis, the complex boasts a collection of minor temples in addition to three principal monuments: the Kiosk of Trajan, Temple of Hathor and Temple of Isis. It's an intensely romantic spot, especially at sunset.

The Sphinx, at the site of the Pyramids of Giza

Cairo & Luxor

Cairo

Home to over 16 million inhabitants, Cairo and its environs are a teeming mass of humanity that seduce many a traveller with chaotic corners, exotic alleyways and fascinating history. The city is easy to combine in a two-centre package with Luxor.

THINGS TO SEE & DO

Khan al-Khalili

Cairo's fascinating souk, in the heart of the Islamic quarter, has existed since the 14th century. Today, the Khan is a huge conglomeration of shops selling everything under the sun – even magic spells! Enjoy a *sheesha* (pipe) and a Turkish coffee at Fishawi's Coffeehouse, which has been open continuously for the past 200 years in the centre of all the action.

Museum of Egyptian Antiquities

More than 120,000 relics and antiquities from every period of ancient Egyptian history are housed in this museum. The collection was first gathered under one roof by the French archaeologist Auguste Mariette in 1858 and transferred to its current location in 1902. Exhibits are arranged chronologically from the Old Kingdom to the Roman Empire, with the most popular room being the Tutankhamun Gallery. Try to go first thing in the morning to avoid the crowds. ⓐ Midan El Tahir
ⓣ 202 578 24 52 ⓑ 09.00–18.45 daily

Pyramids of Giza

One of the Seven Wonders of the World, the Pyramids of Giza represent Egypt like no other sight in the country. Built by three successive Pharaohs, they were already more than 2,500 years old by the time of the birth of Jesus Christ. ⓑ 08.00–17.00 daily (till 24.00 in summer)

Luxor

Often combined as part of a two-centre holiday with Hurghada, Luxor (once known as Thebes) was the glittering capital of the Egyptian kingdom during the 18th and 19th Dynasties. At the height of its glory, it had a population as high as one million. Packed with historical interest, Luxor is a convenient gateway for both the Red Sea coast and Nile cruises.

THINGS TO SEE & DO

Temple of Karnak

The Karnak site covers a huge area. Dedicated to the god Amun, the complex is actually composed of several temples, with most visitors focusing their attentions on the massive, central place of worship – the Temple of Amun.

A vast open-air museum, it is the largest ancient religious site in the world, added to continually from its founding during the Middle Kingdom to the 25th Dynasty, 1,300 years later. Sound-and-light shows are held daily, but these are packed with special effects, and may not be to everyone's taste. 🕒 08.00–17.30 daily (till 16.30 in winter)

Valley of the Kings

The Valley of the Kings is an oven of white sand containing 62 tombs, almost all belonging to pharaohs of the 18th, 19th and 20th Dynasties (1570–1090 BC). The tombs were cut into the soft limestone by workmen living in nearby Deir el Medina. Construction and decoration began as soon as a pharaoh came to the throne.

Three corridors lead to an antechamber connecting to a main hall with a sunken floor for receiving the sarcophagus. For fans of King Tutankhamun, it was here that his tomb was famously discovered by Howard Carter in 1922.

Excavations and restoration are constant in the valley, and tombs are open on a rotating schedule. Check in advance with your tour guide or hotel to confirm that the tomb you want to see will be open on the day.

Temple of Karnak

Nile cruise

A cruise is the perfect way to see the wonders of the River Nile and to explore the many ancient monuments and fascinating sights along the way. Nowadays cruises only run between Luxor and Aswan, usually lasting three to five days.

The cruise

Abydos Ancient Abydos was the shrine of Osiris, the god of the underworld. The 19th-Dynasty New Kingdom Pharaoh Seti I built the complex at Abydos as part of a drive to reinstate a sense of Egyptian style popularised during the Old Kingdom.

Dendera Buses will meet your boat to take you to the Ptolemaic Temple of Hathor at Dendera. The drive takes around ten minutes through the outskirts of the town of Qena.

Edfu The present town of Edfu, on the west bank of the Nile, is spread upon the mound of the ancient city of Djeba. Here, according to myth, Horus avenged the murder of his father Osiris by defeating Seth in titanic combat. To mark this triumph of good over evil, a succession of shrines was built here from earliest dynastic times, culminating in the Ptolemaic **Temple of Horus** on the west side of town.

Esna Until the end of the 19th century, Esna was a port of call for camel caravans crossing the desert from the Sudan. The focal point of the town is the **Temple of Khnum**, which is still in the process of being excavated. However, not all cruise boats stop at or visit Esna.

Spices for sale at the local market

LIFESTYLE
Egyptian delights

Food & drink

LOCAL FOOD

The cuisine of Egypt is drawn from all over the Middle East. Very few dishes can claim to be unique to the country – not a surprise considering the country's history of occupation by foreign empires, and its location.

Approximately half of the dishes found in Egyptian kitchens have roots in Turkey, with Lebanon accounting for much of the rest. There are a few exceptions. Coptic Christians claim to have 'invented' *fuul*, *ta'amiya* and *molokhiya*, the making of which is said to be depicted in Pharaonic tomb paintings.

Egyptian cuisine is the food of the people – basic, filling and cheap. While it isn't fashionable, it is tasty and worth exploring.

STAPLES

Fuul and *ta'amiya* are the most common form of fast food found throughout the country. *Fuul* is made from small beans soaked overnight, boiled, then mashed. The result is a paste that is drizzled with olive oil, lemon juice, salt, pepper and cumin. In a restaurant, pickled vegetables and slices of pitta usually will be served alongside this dish free of charge. *Ta'amiya* consists of mashed chickpeas and spices fried in a patty, stuffed in a pitta and served with *tahini* and salad. Travellers may know it better as falafel.

Most establishments dishing up *fuul* and *ta'amiya* also serve *shawarma* (the Egyptian version of the doner kebab) and *kushari* (a dish of rice, lentils, chickpeas, noodles and spices).

MEZE

Meze, a tradition of dining on lots of small dishes and found primarily in Lebanese cuisine, isn't as popular in Egypt as it is in other Middle Eastern nations. There are, however, plenty of tasty Egyptian 'side orders' that would be considered part of a traditional meze platter.

Mahshi consists of vine leaves or various vegetables, such as aubergines, stuffed with minced meat, rice, onions, pine nuts and herbs.

Once stuffed, the vegetable is baked and served piping hot. Another tasty option is *babaghanoug*, made from mashed grilled aubergines.

If you are willing to broaden your taste buds' horizons, you may want to nibble on some offal. *Kibda firekh* (chicken livers) are much loved by locals. You'll know if you've been served a good example if they taste and look like pâté. *Mokh* (brains) are also often dished up, yet are rarely sampled by Western travellers. They are served crumbled and deep-fried, garnished with salad.

For those with truly iron-clad stomachs, lamb's testicles are considered a delicacy and are usually served as part of a mixed grill.

MAIN DISHES

The two most popular main courses in Egypt are *kofta* and kebab. *Kofta* draws its roots from Turkey. It is minced meat, usually shaped into a ball, flavoured with spices and grilled. Kebab is skewered and grilled chunks of meat – usually lamb. Chicken is also sometimes available. The meat is served on a bed of parsley with tomatoes and onions. Bread, tahini and salad are usually added on the side.

Other main options include *firekh* (chicken roasted on a spit, grilled or stewed), ordered by the half or quarter. For a picnic lunch, takeaway spit-roasted chickens are available from many eateries for between E£15 and E£25, depending on weight.

Hamam (pigeon) is a common delicacy, served stuffed with spices and rice. It can also be dished up in a stew, known as *tagen*, which is cooked in a deep clay pot with onions, cracked wheat, rice and tomatoes.

In the Sinai and Red Sea resorts, fish is commonly available, usually grilled simply and served with salad or chips. Try it baked in rock salt for a flavourful experience.

DESSERTS & SWEETS

Desserts in Egypt are invariably sweet and overwhelmingly sticky. Give an Egyptian something that would send most average folk into diabetic shock and they'll devour it with glee.

Baklava, a pastry made from wafer-thin layers of filo filled with crushed nuts, pistachios and covered in honey or syrup, is the most common treat. *Kunafa* is another option made by sieving liquid batter onto a sizzling metal sheet so that it sets in vermicelli-like strands. These are quickly removed so that the dough remains soft and placed on top of soft, sweet cheese or cream. This dessert is most commonly associated with Ramadan.

If you aren't a fan of pastry, don't fret! *Muhallabiya* is thickened milk and rice cream often flavoured with rose water and sprinkled with chopped nuts or coconut. *Um Ali* combines the taste sensations of thickened milk cream with sweetened pastry layers for the ultimate sticky treat.

DRINKS

Shai (tea) and *ahwa* (coffee) are commonly drunk by almost everyone. When ordering tea, make sure to tell your waiter to serve it with either no sugar (*min ghayr sukar*) or a little sugar (*sukar shwaiya*), otherwise it will come heaped with sweetness. An even more refreshing possibility is to drink your tea with mint leaves. This is only offered in season. Ask for *shai na'na'*.

Coffee drinkers should always specify that they want filtered coffee when placing an order. Not to do so will result in the presentation of thick, Turkish coffee. Seasoned drinkers love the stuff; others find it strong and gritty. Resembling espresso in consistency and size, it is an extremely powerful concoction and comes in various levels of sweetness. Unless you have tried it before, you should try it served 'medium sweet'. Beware – do not drink the entire cup as the bottom third contains the coffee grounds!

In hotter months, hot drinks are often shunned in favour of more refreshing tipples. *Karkadai* is an iced beverage made from boiled hibiscus leaves and either lemon juice or yoghurt. You'll recognise it by its distinctive, bright red colour.

In winter, warm your toes with *yansoon*, an aniseed drink preferred by Egyptian mothers for its reputed medical benefits, or *sahlab*, a warm drink made from semolina powder, chopped nuts and milk.

BEER & WINE

As Egypt is a Muslim nation, alcohol selection can be limited – especially during Ramadan. 'Stella' is the most common beer drunk by the Egyptian population, but not the Stella that you may be familiar with. Stella has been brewed in Egypt for over a century and can be bought in small or large cans or bottles. Also for sale is a light brew known as Stella Meister, and a rather stronger version called Sakara, which comes in two strengths, Gold and King. Heineken beer is also brewed in Egypt and can be bought at a higher price.

The Egyptian wine business was for some years in the doldrums, but now things are looking up. Local wine comes in many varieties, some better than others. Choose from a fairly large range of white, rosé and red wines including Shahrazade, Grand Marquis, Omar Khyyam, Obelisk, Pharaohs, Château des Rêves (red only) and Cape Bay Chardonnay. All are reasonably palatable, especially the white Shahrazade. Don't be surprised during the hot summer months if your red wine is served chilled to stop it going off.

VEGETARIANS

If you are vegetarian, you won't find it particularly difficult sticking to it – but you might be bored. The staple foods of *fuul* and *ta'amiya* are perfect for your palate, as well as such meze dishes as hummus, tahini and *babaghanoug*. After that, the list of options dies fast.

Egyptians find it difficult to understand the concept of vegetarianism. In order to get your point across, say *ana nabaatee* (I'm a vegetarian) (if you are male) or *ana nabatiya* (if you are female) to your waiter. Be warned: any dish that says it is vegetarian may be dubbed that because it consists mainly of vegetables, but it may also have chunks of meat, so ask first.

Menu decoder

Here are some of the authentically Egyptian dishes that you might encounter in local eateries and restaurants.

Asabeeh Rolled filo pastry filled with pistachio, honey, pine and cashew nuts
Babaghanoug Aubergine paste, sometimes mashed with tahini
Baklava Flaky filo pastry filled with honey and nuts
Balila Milk dish with nuts, raisins and wheat
Barazak Flat, circular cookies sprinkled with sesame seeds
Basbousa Pastry of semolina, honey and nuts
Börek Triangles of light pastry stuffed with salty white cheese, spinach or minced meat
Fasoolyeh Green-bean stew
Fatir A dish, similar to a pancake or pizza, made of layers of filo pastry with sweet or savoury fillings
Fattoush Salad of toasted bread, tomatoes, onions and mint leaves
Firekh Chicken roasted on a spit, grilled or stewed
Fuul Broad (fava) beans served with oil and lemon, sometimes also with onions, meat, eggs or tomato sauce
Hamam Pigeon, usually baked or grilled and served stuffed with rice and spices
Hummus Chickpea paste mixed with tahini, garlic and lemon, sometimes served with pine nuts and/or meat. Hummus is actually the Arabic for 'chickpea' and is more commonly used to refer to this in Egypt
Isfinjiya Coconut slice
Kebab Chunks of lamb grilled with onions and tomatoes
Kibbeh Minced lamb, bulgur wheat and pine nuts shaped into a patty and deep-fried
Kibbeh nayeh Minced lamb and cracked wheat served raw like steak tartare
Kibda Chicken liver sautéed in lemon or garlic
Kofta Minced meat flavoured with spices and onions, grilled on a skewer

Kunafa Vermicelli-like strands of cooked batter over a creamy sweet cheese base baked in syrup

Kushari Spicy mixture of noodles, lentils, chickpeas and rice topped with fried onions and a tomato sauce

Labneh A cheesy yoghurt paste, which is often heavily flavoured with garlic or mint

Loubieh French bean salad with tomatoes, onions and garlic

Mahshi A variety of vegetables (peppers, tomatoes, aubergines, courgettes) filled with minced meat, rice, herbs and pine nuts

Makarona Macaroni 'cake' basked in a white sauce or minced meat gravy

Molokhiya Jew's mallow, a leafy vegetable stewed with meat or chicken broth and garlic to make a dish that resembles slimy spinach

Muhallabiya Sweet rice or cornflour pudding, topped with pistachios

Mushabbak Lace-shaped pastry drenched in syrup

Muttabel Similar to *babaghanoug*, but the blended aubergine is mixed with tahini, yoghurt and olive oil to achieve a creamier consistency

Samak mashwi Grilled fish served with salad, bread and chips

Shakshouka Chopped meat and tomato sauce, cooked with an egg on top

Shanklish Salad of small pieces of crumbled, tangy, strong cheese mixed with chopped onion and tomato

Shawarma Slivers of pressed, spit-roasted lamb, served in pitta bread

Ta'amiya Balls of deep-fried mashed chickpeas and spices

Tabbouleh Salad of bulgur wheat, parsley, sesame seeds, tomato, lemon and garlic

Tahini Sesame seed paste mixed with spices, garlic and lemon, eaten with pitta bread

Um Ali Pastry layers soaked in milk, sugar and nuts, served hot

Wara einab Vine leaves filled with spiced minced meat and flavoured with lemon juice

Zalabiya Pastries dipped in rose water

Shopping

ALABASTER

Vases, statuettes and ashtrays are often carved from alabaster. All too often you will be pestered by touts offering alabaster 'antiquities'. Most are two a penny, so if you like what you see then make an offer of approximately one tenth of the asking price.

ANTIQUITIES

Any antiquity you are offered is bound to be fake. There are some Pharaonic, Coptic and Islamic artefacts available on the market, but they will be much more expensive than anything found on the street. It is illegal to export genuine antiquities without government approval.

BOOKS & PRINTS

Books on Egypt and Egyptology are a wonderful souvenir, as well as reproduced prints of works by Egypt-inspired painters such as the 19th-century Scottish artist David Roberts.

BRASS & COPPER

Candlesticks, lamps, mugs and pitchers made from brass are beautiful and functional. If the item is something that you might eat off or drink out of, make sure it is coated with another metal (such as silver), as brass and copper can be highly poisonous when combined with some substances.

CLOTHING & FABRICS

The *galabiya*, a full-length traditional garment worn by Egyptian men, is a popular piece of casual wear for both men and women. Egyptian cotton is a good buy from shops such as New Man and Mobaco and has products for both sexes, whether adults or children.

GLASS

Muski glass, usually turquoise or dark brown and recognisable by its numerous air bubbles, has been handblown in Egypt for centuries.

JEWELLERY

Egyptian jewellery mostly mimics the more obvious Pharaonic motifs such as the scarab (good luck), cartouche, ankh (symbol of life) and the Eye of Horus. Items of Islamic motifs also exist, but are usually confined to hands and eyes used for warding off evil.

Other items worth considering are strands of turquoise or Bedouin silverwork.

LEATHERWORK, SHOES & ACCESSORIES

Handbags, belts, suitcases and hassocks are common. Egyptian leather is, however, not of the finest quality.

Nargilehs *make an original souvenir*

MUSICAL INSTRUMENTS

Traditional musical instruments are an intriguing purchase, whether to look at or to play. Options include the *oud* (lute), *rabab* (viol), *nai* (flute), *kanoon* (dulcimer), *tabla* (drum), *mismare baladi* (oboe) and *duf* (tambourine).

NARGILEHS

Sometimes known as a 'hubbly-bubbly' or *sheesha*, a *nargileh* is a water pipe traditionally used to smoke sweet apple tobacco. The best *nargilehs* will have glass rather than brass bodies for holding the water.

PAPYRUS

Sheets of papyrus with Pharaonic scenes painted on them are often made from banana leaves. To determine if you are purchasing the 'real thing', there is an easy test. Real papyrus can withstand being crumpled up. Banana leaves will crack if you attempt to bend them.

SCENTS & SPICES

Egypt has been one of the world's greatest centres for spice trading and perfume essences for thousands of years. Almost every souk will have a plethora of stalls selling an array of colourful powders and scents.

WEAVINGS, CARPETS & TAPESTRIES

Egypt is not well known for its carpets or weaving traditions. You can sometimes find decent rugs produced from neighbouring countries or Bedouin weavings.

WOODWORK & INLAY

Wooden trays, chess boards and boxes intricately inlaid with mother-of-pearl and coloured bits of wood are surprisingly affordable. If you have the dosh, you may even consider investing in a *mashrabiya* – a carved wooden screen found in many traditional homes.

Children

Egyptians are extremely indulgent towards children, sometimes overly so. You may have to politely sweep your child away from the embracing arms and lips as well as continuous mobile phone snapshots. You will find that your children will receive a warm welcome wherever you go, including mosques, archaeological sites, fine hotels and restaurants.

You will need to be extra careful near excavation sites as they have no warning tape around them. Traffic lights are few and far between, making street crossings perilous too.

The unrelenting sun can cause havoc on a child's skin. Always make sure your child is carefully protected with sunblock that is reapplied each time they come out of the water. Long-sleeve clothing, hats and sunglasses are also highly recommended.

If you want some time alone, better hotels will usually provide child-minders, and private medical services are good if you need to see a doctor.

Children may well take more readily to the strangeness of the environment than you do, and they will probably find the scent and the bustle of a bazaar more interesting than a museum. Carriage or camel rides and sailing excursions are particular favourites.

TOP ACTIVITIES

Aquarium

Hurghada has a small and very poorly funded aquarium that is worth a visit if your child wants to see 'Nemo' but is either too young or lacks the swimming skills needed to snorkel or dive. Be warned – the tanks are very small and some of the fish are not in the best of health. ⓐ Corniche, Ad-Dahar ⓣ 065 354 85 57 ⓛ 09.00–23.00 daily ⓘ Admission charge

Camel rides

Camel journeys led by Bedouin guides are very popular with kids. Many include Bedouin tea or dinner, which your child may not be so keen to try. Endeavour to arrange your trip with Bedouin guides in order to ensure authenticity and secure a good price.

WATERSPORTS
When letting your child go off for a swim, it is best to keep your eye on them at all times. Public beaches do not have lifeguards of any sort, while private resort coverage can be sketchy. Tides can be powerful and may challenge even good swimmers.

Dolphin House

A large school of dolphins lives in an area north of Hurghada called Dolphin House. You can go out on a boat to see them or swim with them. Great fun for children.

Submarine rides

Sindbad Submarine in Hurghada offers rides that are very popular with adventurous kids, allowing families to plumb the depths, yet remain dry. The submarines accommodate up to 46 people per ride and carry passengers down as low as 22 m (72 ft) below sea level. The trip lasts two hours, of which an hour is spent on a boat travelling to the site from the Sindbad Beach Resort. Bookings can be made at a number of hotels in town and also at the **Sindbad**. ⓣ 065 344 96 01 ⓘ Admission charge

ⓘ If it is a really scorching hot day, there are many things to do indoors, or in the evening, when the heat of the sun has gone. Also, try to ensure that children wear protective covering on their heads – and it's not a bad idea for grown-ups to do the same!

Sports & activities

As could be expected, sports and activities in the Red Sea resorts revolve mainly around water. Sharm el-Sheikh is widely considered to be one of the world's finest diving centres, while Hurghada is well known for its windsurfing.

Deep-sea fishing

Day trips can be arranged in a number of resort towns. It is usually best to book two to three days in advance to avoid disappointment. The cost of a full-day excursion is about £210–250 (US$340–400) per boat including lunch and equipment. **Sport n' Fun** ⓐ Steigenberger Golf Resort, El Gouna ⓣ 012 380 74 30

Desert adventures

Dahab and Marsa Shagra are wonderful spots from which to join hikes, jeep and camel safaris into the desert.

Dahab Embah Safari Tours ⓣ 069 364 16 90 ⓦ www.embah.com; King Safari Dahab ⓣ 069 364 23 84 ⓦ www.kingsafaridahab.com

Marsa Shagra Red Sea Desert Adventures ⓣ 012 399 38 60 ⓦ www.redseadesertadventures.com ⓘ Oct–Mar only

Diving

The Red Sea resorts of Egypt became famous as holiday destinations primarily due to the excellent diving conditions of the region. Ask your tour rep and/or hotel concierge in order to determine who the best diving operators are in town. If in doubt, sit at any of the waterside cafés and strike up a conversation with a few of the expat divers in order to get advice.

Paragliding & waterskiing

Paragliding and waterskiing are available at a limited number of centres. Make sure to check the quality of the equipment and establish the reputation of the operator before you decide to try it out.

❶ Check your insurance – it may not cover either sport unless you select an 'adventure sports' option

Public beaches

Most public beaches are extremely untidy and will bring unwanted attention from a cross-section of the Egyptian population. Private beaches offer the best options. Many hotels and resorts open their beaches to outsiders for a fee. Don't think about trying to sneak past security as paying guests are always given distinctively coloured towels to separate them from outsiders, or you might be asked to produce your room key or give your room number.

Snorkelling

Snorkelling is a great option for those who are wary of diving, yet still want to witness the incredible undersea life in the Red Sea. It is also much more affordable if you are on a tight budget.

Bobo's Watersports ⓐ Sharm el-Sheikh (ⓣ 069 360 09 31)
Emperor Divers ⓐ Hurghada (ⓣ 012 234 09 95)
Sun 'n' Fun ⓐ Sharm el-Sheikh (ⓣ 069 366 11 13)

Thrills & chills

Go-kart racing, bungee rockets and trampolining are some of the more adventurous activities available in El Gouna, Hurghada and Sharm el-Sheikh. Bookings can be made via your concierge.

Windsurfing

Powerful gusts make Hurghada and Dahab great choices if you are an avid windsurfer. Many resorts have watersports centres where you can rent boards and wetsuits. Ask at your hotel for the better centres.

Festivals & events

MUSLIM HOLIDAYS & EVENTS

Muslims follow a lunar calendar, resulting in varying festival dates. However, they happen in the following order:

Ramadan

During this month of fasting, practised by all Muslims, except for children and pregnant women, nothing is permitted to pass the lips between sunrise and sunset. After dark, however, more food is consumed in Egypt during this month than at any other time of year. When the sun sets, families and friends gather and the evening takes on a carnival atmosphere – an excellent time to explore the streets.

Eid el-Fitr

This three-day festival marking the end of Ramadan is the biggest party of the year. Family members from abroad will often fly in to celebrate.

Eid el-Adha (Quarban Bairam)

This feast celebrates Abraham's willingness to sacrifice Isaac. It occurs in the month when the haj, or annual pilgrimage, takes place. If an Egyptian has the funds, they will purchase a sheep for the feast, slaughter it and distribute portions to celebrate the occasion.

Ras el-Sana el-Hegira

The Islamic New Year begins on the first day of the month of Muharram. Koranic and other religious texts are read at this time.

Muslim & Christian *moulids*

A *moulid* is a festival in honour of a holy man. It usually takes on the characteristics of a medieval fair with popular entertainments and a souk. The only national *moulid* is the Moulid el-Nabi in honour of the Prophet's birthday on the 12th day of Rabei el Awal. Most *moulids* are very local events celebrated by just a single town or village.

WHIRLING DERVISHES

Mevlana, the 13th-century Sufi master who founded his sect at Konya in Turkey, also has followers in Egypt. Often banned in other Muslim countries, whirling dervishes strive to achieve mystical union with God through ecstatic whirling.

NON-MUSLIM HOLIDAYS & EVENTS

New Year's Day 1 January.
Christmas 7 January – Coptic Christmas is a low-key holiday only celebrated by Coptics. Coptic businesses close for the day.
Easter March/April – The most important Coptic holiday. All other businesses remain open.
Sham el-Nessim March/April – This national holiday, celebrated by Egyptians of all faiths, falls on the first Monday after Coptic Easter and is considered a 'salute to spring', with picnics and family gatherings.
Sinai Liberation Day 25 April – Official national holiday celebrating Israel's return of Sinai in 1982.
May Day 1 May – Official national holiday.
Revolution Day 23 July – Official national holiday commemorating the date of the 1952 coup when the Free Officers seized power.
National Day 6 October – Official national holiday celebrating Egyptian successes during the 1973 war with Israel.

International fishing tournament

Held at Hurghada and attended by anglers from all over the world, this tournament, in February, is a must for fans of deep-sea fishing.

South Sinai camel festival

Hundreds of sellers come from across the Middle East to sell prize camels, but the real fun is watching the animals race to the finish line.

A beach sign in Sinai

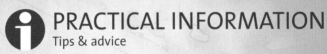

PRACTICAL INFORMATION

Tips & advice

Accommodation

While Cairo now offers decent middle-category accommodation, it is best to go with the upper end of the market in the Red Sea.

All prices are for a double room, per night, based on double occupancy.

££ under E£1,000
£££ over E£1,000

Coraya Beach Iberotel ££ This environmentally friendly hotel is built in the Moorish style and located on a secluded beach, ideal for exploring the wonderful reefs and marine life. Good for families as well as individuals. ⓐ Madinat Coraya, Marsa Alam ⓣ 065 375 00 00 ⓦ www.iberotel.com ⓔ info@iberotelcorayabeach.com

Hilton Nuweiba Coral Resort ££ This is a peaceful resort, ideal for relaxing or being active with tennis, mini-golf and volleyball on offer as well as diving and watersports. Either stay in a room with a balcony or choose a bungalow with sea views. ⓐ Nuweiba, South Sinai ⓣ 069 352 03 20 ⓦ www.hilton.com ⓔ ali.hassan@hilton.com

Hyatt Regency Hotel ££ With the mountains as a backdrop and the sea on the doorstep, the Hyatt Regency is a stylish hotel with unique architecture and elegant guest rooms. Everything you could want is at hand, even a desert campsite in the nearby mountains for starlit dining. ⓐ Taba Heights, Sinai ⓣ 069 358 02 34 ⓦ www.taba.regency.hyatt.com ⓔ taba@hyattintl.com

Oricana Hotel ££ A three-star budget hotel located in the centre of Dahab and close to the sea. All rooms are comfortably furnished, with minibar, air conditioning, en-suite shower and toilet, plus private balcony. There is also a small pool and restaurant facilities. ⓐ Mashraba, Dahab ⓣ 069 364 25 01/2 ⓦ www.oricanahotel.com

Sheraton Miramar Resort ££ Set on nine islands in beautifully landscaped gardens, the Sheraton Miramar is a stylish resort hotel right on the sandy beach of El Gouna. Facilities include two swimming pools, three restaurants and a number of bars. ⓐ El Gouna, Red Sea ⓣ 065 354 56 06 ⓦ www.sheratonmiramarresort.com

Sheraton Soma Bay ££ Set on a peninsula with wonderful views, this Pharaonic-style hotel has many amenities including three pools, several restaurants and bars, and all rooms have a balcony or terrace. ⓐ Soma Bay, Red Sea ⓣ 065 354 58 45 ⓦ www.sheraton-somabay.com

Sindbad Beach Resort ££ Centrally located and right on the Red Sea with its own beach, this budget hotel is perfect for those who want to participate in a variety of watersports. Ideal for families, with a lively animation team to keep things upbeat. ⓐ Corniche, Ad-Dahar, Hurghada ⓣ 065 344 32 61 ⓦ www.sindbad-group.com ⓔ sindbadhrg@red-sea.com

Steigenberger Al Dau Beach Resort ££ Impressive hotel overlooking its own sandy beach with comfortable and elegant rooms. Its main feature is a huge pool interspersed with islands and bridges and a river meandering through the resort. ⓐ Youssif Afifi Road, Sigala, Hurghada ⓣ 065 346 54 00 ⓦ www.steigenbergeraldaubeach.com

Camel Hotel ££–£££ Located in the heart of Na'ama Bay's pedestrian area, this award-winning diving hotel is a great option for families or individuals. A swimming pool, restaurants, cafés, bars and the diving centre are all on the spot. ⓐ Na'ama Bay, Sharm el-Sheikh ⓣ 069 360 07 00 ⓦ www.cameldive.com ⓔ info@cameldive.com

Makadi Beach Iberotel ££–£££ A lovely resort hotel located directly on the beach and part of a delightful holiday complex within easy reach of shops, restaurants, dive centre, disco, spa and health club. ⓐ Madinat Makadi, Makadi Bay ⓣ 065 359 00 00 ⓦ www.iberotel.com ⓔ info@iberotelmakadibeach.com

Preparing to go

GETTING THERE

The cheapest way to get to Egypt's Red Sea resorts is to book a package holiday with one of the leading tour operators.

By air

Egypt has three international airports directly serving the Red Sea resorts (Hurghada, Marsa Alam and Sharm el-Sheikh) and two further major gateways (Cairo, Luxor) which are convenient if a twin-centre holiday is what you are after.

In the event that charter flights prove inconvenient, or you are looking to arrange a bespoke itinerary, the national flag carrier is EgyptAir. The airline flies throughout the country from its Cairo base and internationally throughout Europe, Africa, Asia and North America. However, EgyptAir isn't renowned for being a particularly good airline when it comes to service, although efforts to improve are being made. British charter flights are usually more enjoyable and better priced.

Many people are aware that air travel emits CO_2, which contributes to climate change. You may be interested in the possibility of lessening the environmental impact of your flight through the charity **Climate Care**, which offsets your CO_2 by funding environmental projects around the world. Visit Ⓦ www.climatecare.org

TOURISM AUTHORITIES

Further information about Egypt can be obtained from the **Egyptian Tourist Authority**. ⓐ 170 Piccadilly, London W1J 9EJ ⓣ 020 7493 5283. Useful information can also be found on the **Egyptian National Tourist Organisation** site. Ⓦ www.touregypt.net

BEFORE YOU LEAVE

It is not necessary to have inoculations to travel to Egypt, but you should make sure you and your family are up to date with the basics, such as tetanus and polio. If you are travelling beyond the Red Sea coast to locations in southern Egypt or sub-Saharan Africa, meningitis and typhoid vaccinations are a must.

It is always a good idea to pack a small first-aid kit to carry with you. Sunblock is more expensive in Egypt than it is in the UK, so it is worth bringing your own. If you are taking prescription medicines, ensure that you pack enough for the duration of your visit.

Check that your insurance policy covers you adequately for loss of possessions and valuables, for activities you might want to try – such as scuba diving, horse riding or watersports – and for emergency medical and dental treatment, including flights home if required.

ENTRY FORMALITIES

Visitors to Egypt require a visa to enter the country. Citizens of most countries, including the UK, Ireland, the US, Canada and Australia, can obtain tourist visas on arrival in the country if landing at Cairo, Luxor or Hurghada airports. Visas obtained on arrival are valid for one month from the date of entry.

If you are planning a longer stay, or are arriving at Aswan, Suez or Nuweiba, you will have to get your visa from an Egyptian embassy or consulate. Visas obtained from an embassy are valid for three months and cost £15. The **Egyptian embassy** in the UK is located at ⓐ 26 South Street, London W1K 1DW ⓣ 020 7499 3304/2401

MONEY

Egypt's basic unit of currency is the Egyptian pound, which is divided into 100 *piastres* and can be written as EGP or E£. There is a new E£1 coin, in addition to coins for 5pt, 10pt, 20pt, 25pt and 50pt. Banknotes are written in Arabic on one side and English on the reverse. These come in denominations of 25pt and 50pt, and in E£1, E£5, E£10, E£20, E£50, E£100 and E£200. Always keep a supply of as many small bills as possible as finding change for larger denominations can sometimes be a challenge.

Cash machines taking major bank cards can be found almost everywhere, although sometimes it is difficult to withdraw money from them for various reasons including power fluctuation and computer error. In case your card should be swallowed by the machine, record your card number and emergency telephone numbers and inform the bank who has your card as soon as possible. A spare card is a wise precaution and will give you access to emergency funds.

There are numerous bank kiosks offering currency exchange services around the clock at every airport in the country. Traveller's cheques are the safest way to carry money as money will be refunded if the cheques are lost or stolen. You may be asked to show a copy of the bank receipt you got when you purchased them – and also your passport – so make sure you carry these with you at all times.

CLIMATE

Average daytime temperatures in Red Sea resorts range from 20°C (68°F) in January to 32°C (90°F) in July.

You will often find temperatures vary greatly over the course of the day and can reach as high as 50°C (122°F) in hot years. This is due to the dryness of the air and the absence of cloud.

BAGGAGE ALLOWANCE

Baggage allowances vary according to the airline, destination and the class of travel, but 23 kg (50 lb) per person is the norm for luggage that is carried in the hold. Charter airlines often have more limited restrictions, so it is best to check your ticket or contact the airline before departing.

You are also allowed one item of cabin baggage weighing no more than 5 kg (11 lb) and measuring 46 by 30 by 23 cm (18 by 12 by 9 in) but, again, this can vary between airlines. In addition, you can usually carry your duty-free purchases, umbrella, handbag, coat and camera as hand baggage. Large items – surfboards, golf clubs, collapsible wheelchairs and pushchairs – are usually charged as extras and it is a good idea to let the airline know in advance that you want to bring these.

During your stay

AIRPORTS

From Hurghada airport the only means of transport to El Gouna is by taxi, taking 35–40 minutes. Taxis wait outside the airport and cost E£90, or E£50 for a public taxi. Hotels can organise transfers too. For Hurghada town centre, expect to pay around E£15.

Marsa Alam's airport does not receive enough flights per day to merit a taxi rank, so drivers only assemble to meet the incoming flights, but you can prebook a shuttle bus.

COMMUNICATIONS

Telephones & Internet

Local and international telephone services are available in most hotels. Local calls can also be made from some kiosks, shops and restaurants. International calls can be made from PTT offices. Normally you pay first for a fixed number of minutes. For assistance, dial ☎ 144/120

If you are thinking of taking your mobile phone to Egypt, it is advisable to check first with your supplier to see if it will work.

Internet cafés exist in most towns and cities, and many hotels have Internet access or Wi-Fi.

Post offices

Post between Egypt and foreign countries can be efficient as long as you use letter boxes at a major hotel or central post office. Some letter boxes are visited by postal employees only very rarely, if at all. Anything that isn't a simple letter or postcard can take ages. Post offices are open 09.00–14.00 Saturday–Thursday. If in doubt, purchase your stamps at your hotel and ask them to post articles on your behalf.

CUSTOMS

Egyptians are an extremely friendly and welcoming people – as long as you follow a few simple rules. If you are a keen photographer and you wish to take a photograph of a person, you must ask their permission

TELEPHONING ABROAD

To call Egypt from the following countries, dial the codes listed below followed by the eight- or nine-digit number (minus the initial zero).

Australia & New Zealand 00 20
South Africa 00 20
UK & Ireland 00 20
US & Canada 00 20

To call overseas from Egypt, dial 00, then the country code then the area code (minus the initial zero) followed by the number.

Australia 00 61
Canada 00 1
Ireland 00 353
New Zealand 00 64
South Africa 00 27
UK 00 44
US 00 1

before doing so, especially in rural, remote communities where taking a photo can actually cause serious offence. Some locals may prevent you from taking a picture if it portrays Egypt in a bad light.

You should also avoid taking any photos of military installations. If a soldier sees you doing so, you could find yourself in seriously hot water.

Photographs are a great way to break the ice with locals. Be sure to bring a collection of family photos as exchanging them can lead to a new-found friendship.

When entering a private home it may be appropriate to remove your shoes as a sign of respect. It is also customary to take a gift.

DRESS CODES

These days shorts are acceptable to wear in the Red Sea and Sinai beach towns – indeed they are quite the norm for both men and women.

However, if you are planning to visit any cultural sites, women should wear trousers, or skirts covering the knee, and tops should cover the shoulders and midriff. Men should wear full-length trousers or at least long shorts and a shirt. Although wearing a hat is not a requirement, it is a good idea to protect you from the sun.

ELECTRICITY

Voltage in Egypt is 220 volts, but you will need a two-pin adaptor to fit Egyptian sockets.

EMBASSIES & CONSULATES

If you find yourself in legal trouble, you have the right to contact your country's embassy or consulate, which are all located in Cairo. They can provide advice and will assist you in obtaining legal help from an English-speaking lawyer but they will not pay for the service. Add a 2 in front of the telephone numbers below when calling from outside Cairo.

Australia ⓐ World Trade Centre, 1191 Corniche El Nil, Boulaq ⓣ 02 2770 66 00
Canada ⓐ 26 Kamel El Shenawy, Garden City ⓣ 02 2791 87 00
Ireland ⓐ 22 Sharia Hassam Assem, Zamalek ⓣ 02 2735 82 64
New Zealand 8th floor, North Tower, Nile City, Corniche El Nil, Boulaq ⓣ 02 2461 60 00
UK ⓐ 7 Sharia Ahmed Ragheb, Garden City ⓣ 02 2791 60 00
US ⓐ 5 Sharia Kamal El Din Salah, Garden City ⓣ 02 2797 33 00

EMERGENCY NUMBERS

For an ambulance or help in an emergency call:
Ambulance ⓣ 123
Fire brigade ⓣ 180
Police ⓣ 122

GETTING AROUND

Driving rules & conditions

In Egypt, you drive on the right. An international driving licence is an absolute must. If you are caught driving without one, you will be subjected to a heavy fine. The official speed limit ranges between 90 and 100 km/h (56–62 mph) outside towns and on major highways, although this is often broken by locals. If you are caught speeding, you may be fined on the spot, your licence will be confiscated and you will have to go to the traffic headquarters in the area to get it back. This is a lengthy process that can ruin a holiday.

Many roads have checkpoints where police will ask for identity papers, so keep your passport and driving licence on-hand to avoid a fine.

Driving is chaotic across the country. There is, however, one rule of the road that is commonly accepted by all: whoever is in front has right of way. If a car is a hair's breadth ahead of you and cuts across your path, you will be liable if you hit it. If you do have an accident, get to the nearest police station as fast as possible to report the incident.

Car hire

Most international car rental firms have offices in Egypt, including Avis, Budget, Europcar, Hertz and Thrifty. Rates are in line with international charges, making a really cheap deal a rare find. No matter which firm you go with, be sure to read every inch of your agreement as terms and conditions can differ wildly. Most rental agreements include insurance and the first 100 km (62 miles) as part of the price package, but it is always wise to check before signing anything. Unlimited mileage options are also available, but should be avoided if you are planning to stick firmly to your resort town as there is often a seven-day minimum.
It is also important to note that any price quoted to you will not include a mandatory 10 to 17 per cent tax added to your final bill.

In order to rent a car, drivers must be over the age of 25. Some companies, such as Europcar, offer the option of a one-way rental from, for example, Sharm el-Sheikh to Cairo. It is also possible to hire a car and driver if you feel unsure about tackling Egyptian roads.

Public transport

In the Red Sea resorts, service taxis are the cheapest option to use if you want to get around. Every town in Egypt has a service taxi station. To use one, find a driver who is going in your direction and get in.

Be warned: service taxi journeys are not the most enjoyable method of transport as the driver won't depart until the entire vehicle is full. If you want a more comfortable trip, you can pay for additional seats to get the car moving. Service taxi drivers often work extraordinarily long hours, so do make sure you find one who looks wide awake to avoid any potential danger.

Taxis in Egypt are extremely cheap and easy to hail. Some taxi drivers may still stop to take on other passengers, although this custom is disappearing with the introduction of metered taxis. Here are a few companies: **Yellow cabs** (air-conditioned) ☎ 19155; **Blue Cab** (air-conditioned, set prices) ☎ 202 3760 96 16. White metered taxis are now replacing old black-and-white ones.

Always have the correct fare in small bills available as the driver will never have any change if they think they can get away with taking a large tip.

HEALTH, SAFETY & CRIME

Medical help

Medical care is not always readily available outside major cities. Even some of the larger resort towns lack full-service facilities and may require you to be sent to Cairo in the event of a major accident or illness.

Pharmacies

Egyptian pharmacies often have English-speaking staff and are very helpful for minor complaints and illnesses. They can provide valuable advice and sell over-the-counter medication and prescription drugs – often costing less than in the UK. Antibiotics, however, are usually much more expensive. Be warned: pharmacies keep erratic hours and may not be open during the hot hours of the afternoon or on weekends (Fridays/Saturdays).

If you are prescribed drugs during your stay due to illness or accident, you should be able to reclaim the cost through your medical insurance. Pharmacies are not like chemist shops in the UK, so you are unlikely to find everything that you might need. You are advised to purchase condoms and feminine sanitary items prior to departure as the quality of these items in Egypt can be far from Western standards.

Most major resorts do sell sunblock, but you will find that the selection of high-factor creams is limited and usually very pricey.

Although not officially recognised but becoming increasingly popular, remedies are available from homeopaths.

Water

It is advisable not to drink tap water anywhere in Egypt. Always stick to bottled water, which is readily available throughout the country. When purchasing your bottle, be sure the top has not been tampered with before drinking. Also check that any ice put in your drinks is made only from purified water.

Precautions

Cooling breezes off the coast can mask the intensity of the sun's rays, which can burn you if deflected off the sand or nearby water. You can even burn in the shade, especially if you have sensitive skin. Keep covered up during the hottest part of the day and drink plenty of water to avoid dehydration.

In order to avoid snake bites, do not walk barefoot or stick your hand into holes or cracks. If bitten, immobilise the bitten limb with a splint and apply a bandage with firm pressure over the wound. Do not apply a tourniquet, cut or suck the bite. Seek medical attention as soon as possible in order to receive the necessary antivenom.

Mosquitoes can be a nuisance but are easily dealt with by burning insect coils or using an electric deterrent. Malaria is not carried by mosquitoes in the Red Sea coastal areas; however, dengue fever is a remote possibility.

Crime

Egypt is generally safe. Nevertheless, take special care with passports, tickets and money. Hotels will look after your valuables for you, but you should obtain a receipt. If the property has in-room safe facilities, use them. Be sure to keep a close eye on your valuables when travelling on public transport as pickpocketing can be a problem.

Police

The police have a high profile in Egypt. In fact, Cairo has more police officers per capita than any other city in the world. There are many different police forces, each with a separate and distinct area of responsibility. Tourist police are where you should report thefts and receive documents for insurance purposes.

Restricted areas

Avoid any military bases and take heed of all signs near them. Failure to do so could result in your arrest. Never take any photographs of airports, highways, government buildings or commercial ports.

MEDIA

There are a few English-language newspapers, the rather thin daily *Egyptian Gazette* (the *Egyptian Mail* on Saturdays), the *Daily News Egypt* and the more weighty *Al-Ahram Weekly* published every Thursday.

English newspapers are quite easy to find but are usually a day or two late and can be bought at vastly inflated prices.

CNN, BBC World, Euronews and other foreign channels are available in almost all major resorts.

OPENING HOURS

Traditional shopping hours in Egypt are 10.00–22.00 with shorter hours on Sundays, except perhaps in heavily touristed areas. Many shops close on Fridays, and some also close on Sundays.

Banks are usually open 08.30–14.00 Sunday to Thursday. A very few open in the evenings – 17.00–20.00 in winter or 18.00–21.00 in summer.

During the month of Ramadan, shop hours are severely reduced, with many establishments only open 10.30–15.30 and 20.00–22.00.

RELIGION

About 90 per cent of Egypt's population is Muslim. While Islam prevails in Egyptian culture, very few pray the specified five times a day. Friday noon is the exception, when almost every male in the country heeds the call to prayer. The remaining 10 per cent of the population is Coptic Christian. The two populations live in relatively peaceful coexistence.

If you visit a mosque, always make sure to remove your shoes before entering.

TIME DIFFERENCES

Egypt is two hours ahead of the UK and one hour ahead of Central European Time. Clocks go forward one hour on the last Friday in April and back one hour in October.

TIPPING

Tipping, otherwise known as *baksheesh*, is common practice in Egypt. A tip will be required (if not expected) to get anything done, no matter how small. The basic rule is to offer *baksheesh* only in return for a service, and not to pay until the service has been performed. Resist any forms of intimidation, especially from children who may pester you.

TOILETS

Apart from better hotels and restaurants, toilets will be of poor standard. Never count on there being toilet paper and, if there is, you will probably have to place used sheets in a bin.

TRAVELLERS WITH DISABILITIES

Egypt is sadly lacking in facilities for travellers with mobility problems. Ramps are non-existent, public buildings are difficult to enter and manoeuvre, and kerbs are extremely high. Despite this, you will find that locals are keen to assist you if you get into difficulty.

ACKNOWLEDGEMENTS
Thomas Cook Publishing wishes to thank the photographers, picture libraries and other organisations, to whom the copyright belongs, for the photographs in this book.

BIG STOCK PHOTO K Avraham page 13, V Pomortzeff page 55; DREAMSTIME L Dean page 61, Enjoylife25 page 63, C Garrow page 39, Lenkusa page 76, C Loffonseca page 21, J Patava page 66, S Peeters page 26, V Pomortzeff page 78, P Prescott page 111, S Privezentseva page 90, slava 296 page 59, Ursula1964 page 31; EGYPTIAN NATIONAL TOURIST AUTHORITY pages 10–11, 73, 83; THOMAS COOK pages 5, 9, 36, 71, 84, 87, 88, 93, 95; A Tiernan pages 42, 103; WORLD PICTURES/PHOTOSHOT pages 16, 46

For CAMBRIDGE PUBLISHING MANAGEMENT LIMITED:
Project editor: Kate Taylor
Layout: Paul Queripel
Proofreaders: Sara Chare & Karolin Thomas

Send your thoughts to
books@thomascook.com

- **Found a beach bar, peaceful stretch of sand or must-see sight that we don't feature?**
- **Like to tip us off about any information that needs a little updating?**
- **Want to tell us what you love about this handy little guidebook and more importantly how we can make it even handier?**

Then here's your chance to tell all! Send us ideas, discoveries and recommendations today and then look out for your valuable input in the next edition of this title.

Email to the above address or write to:
pocket guides Series Editor, Thomas Cook Publishing, PO Box 227, Coningsby Road, Peterborough PE3 8SB, UK.

Useful phrases

Arabic is a challenging language for English-speakers to learn, but if you fancy trying out a bit of Arabic, here are some useful words and phrases with an approximate English pronunciation.

': this sound is a throaty 'a' produced at the back of the throat
": this sound is a guttural stop
/: indicates talking to masc./fem.

English	*Approx pronunciation*
BASICS	
Yes	*na'am*
No	*la"*
Please	*lau samaht/samahti; min fadlak/fadlik*
Thank you	*shukran*
Hello	*"ahlan; "ahlan wa sahlan*
Goodbye	*salaamu 'aleekum; ma'as-salamaama; salaam*
Excuse me, pardon	*'an iznak/iznik*
I'm sorry	*"ana "aasif/"aasifa*
That's okay	*zany; Tayyib; kwayis*
Do you speak English?	*tatakallam/tatakallamiy inglizee?*
Good morning	*sabah al-khayr*
Good afternoon/evening	*masa" al-khayr*
Good night	*tisbah 'ala khayr*
My name is ...	*ismi ...*
NUMBERS	
One	*waahad*
Two	*itnain*
Three	*talaata*
Four	*arba'a*
Five	*khamsa*
Six	*sitta*
Seven	*saba'a*
Eight	*tamanya*
Nine	*tisa'a*
Ten	*'ashara*
Twenty	*'ishreen*
Fifty	*khamseen*
One hundred	*miya*
MONEY	
I would like to change these traveller's cheques/this currency	*"ariyd "aghayar sheekaat siyaaheeya/fulous*
Where is the nearest ATM?	*wayn aqrab makinat ATM?*
Do you accept credit cards?	*anta bitakhod/anti bitakhodee credit cards'?*